Jarosław Dobrzyński

Colour profiles
Marcelo Ribeiro

Republic F-105 Thunderchief

Published in Poland
in 2018
by STRATUS sp.j.
Skr. Poczt. 123,
27-600 Sandomierz 1
e-mail: office@mmpbooks.biz
www.stratusbooks.pl

for
MMPBooks,
e-mail: office@mmpbooks.biz
© 2018 MMPBooks.
http://www.mmpbooks.biz

ISBN
978-83-65281-79-1

Editor in chief
Roger Wallsgrove

Editorial Team
Bartłomiej Belcarz
Robert Pęczkowski
Artur Juszczak

Scale Plans
Dariusz Karnas

Colour Plates
Marcelo Ribeiro

DTP
Bartłomiej Belcarz

Printed by
Wydawnictwo
Diecezjalne
i Drukarnia,
www.wds.pl
marketing@wds.pl

PRINTED IN POLAND

Table of contents

To General (Ret.) Donald Kutyna

Acknowledgements

The author would like to thank Mr Donald Kutyna and Mr Anthony Andrews, veteran F-105 pilots of the Vietnam War for their assistance in writing this book, and Mr Krzysztof Radwan, director of Polish Aviation Museum for permission to use photographs from the Museum's collection.

The author would like to dedicate this book to General (Ret.) Donald Kutyna, who flew the only F-105 with a Polish name and markings, whose aircraft and car are now on display at the Polish Aviation Museum, Cracow.

Foreword

The Republic F-105 Thunderchief, commonly known as 'Thud', was one of the most notable combat aircraft of the Cold War era. It was designed to perform one primary role, of supersonic, tactical nuclear bomber to wage war in a major East-West confrontation. Instead, it saw combat in entirely different roles, some of which were not known or even imagined at the moment of its birth, in a conflict which was a spin-off of the Cold War, during which the F-105s flew extremely tough and demanding missions into the fiercest of defences and suffered heavy losses.

The F-105 was the epitome of the US combat aircraft design of the 1950s. It was one of the 'century series' types – supersonic fighter and fighter-bomber jet aircraft, whose designations were in the 100–109 range (the other types of the series to enter service were the North American F-100 Super Sabre, McDonnell F-101 Voodoo, Convair F-102 Delta Dagger, Lockheed F-104 Starfighter and Convair F-106 Delta Dart). The F-105 was the largest and heaviest single-engine, single-seat combat aircraft. Although designated as 'fighter', it was intended exclusively for the air-to-ground role, chiefly nuclear weapons delivery. Its development and early service were plagued by technical problems resulting in crashes, and production was hampered by worker strikes. The name 'Thud' was initially derisive – it was said that this was the sound the plane made when it crashed. Later, when the Thunderchiefs made their mark in Vietnam, the nickname became affectionate. Other nicknames given to the F-105 were 'Ultra Hog', 'Hyper Hog', 'Lead Sled', and 'Flying Anvil' all referring to the aircraft's weight and long take-off roll.

In the history of aerial warfare there are several types of combat aircraft that are associated with one specific conflict or campaign, such as the German Fokker Dr I triplane fighter, which saw combat over the Western Front during the First World War in 1917–1918, Polish PZL P.11c fighter, which defended Poland against overwhelming *Luftwaffe* forces in September 1939, the British Hawker Typhoon fighter-bomber, operating over the Western Front during the Second World War, or the Japanese Mitsubishi A6M Reisen (Zero) fighter, which fought against the Allies in the Far East during the Second World War. The F-105 also belongs to this group – Thunderchiefs flew 75 per cent of all bombing raids on North Vietnam.

When the Vietnam War broke out in 1964, it turned out that of all the USAF's inventory at that time, the F-105 was the most suitable aircraft to conduct strikes on North Vietnam and Laos. This suitability soon proved limited, however: the aircraft was prone to damage and the pilots initially had attacking small attacking small, often mobile and heavily defended targets. This resulted from USAF's priorities of the early Cold War era: nuclear capability was deemed most important. The aircraft's design was optimised for that role and the pilots were also trained primarily for this task. As the war continued, tactics and aircrew skills were refined, but their effectiveness were still hampered by a shortage of proper weaponry, mission limitations imposed by politicians, the convoluted structure of command, and the USAF's personnel policy. Yet the F-105 aircrews did their best, often frustrated by the impression that they were forced to fight with one hand tied behind their backs. Many of them paid the price with their lives, or in long, harsh imprisonment. As the outcome of the war indicated, they had fought for a lost cause, often performing heroic deeds, but their sacrifice was not wasted. The Vietnam War was a bitter lesson for the USAF, from which proper conclusions were drawn, resulting in far better effectiveness and minimised losses in the conflicts that came later.

The combat career of the Thunderchief ended with the Vietnam War. The type remained in service for the next ten years, but being obsolete and war-weary, aircraft were quickly passed to second-line units. Their performance during the Vietnam War gave the USAF new perspective on how important it was to have a tactical strike aircraft, capable of conducting precise attacks on small targets, and what such a type should be like.

Chapter 1
The birth of the F-105

The F-105 was conceived by Alexander Kartveli, an American aircraft designer of Georgian origin, who arrived in the USA in the 1920s. After a brief period with the Fokker/Atlantic Aircraft Company, he met another Russian emigré, Alexander de Seversky. Kartveli became the chief designer in the Seversky Aircraft Corporation, based in Farmingdale, Long Island, New York, which was reorganised as Republic Aviation in 1939. His single-engine fighter designs, the Seversky P-35 and Republic P-43 Lancer evolved into his first true masterpiece – the Republic P-47 Thunderbolt. This was one of the most important fighter aircraft of the Second World War, which excelled both in the air-to-air and ground attack roles. The P-47 was big, heavy, fast and reliable. The pattern was set.

In 1944, when the P-47s fought their fiercest battles in Europe and the Far East, Kartveli commenced work on a new design, powered by turbojet engine. The prototype of the F-84

Alexander Kartveli with models of aircraft he designed. (Republic)

The direct predecessor of the F-105 – Republic RF-84F Thunderflash. (USAF)

An artist's impression of project AP-63-FBX (USAF Museum)

Thunderjet first flew in 1946. Several versions of this fighter-bomber were developed, not all of them successful, but the F-84E and F-84G fared well in combat during the Korean War and served with many NATO and other countries, including Iran and Yugoslavia.

Within just a few years of the first nuclear attacks on Hiroshima and Nagasaki, nuclear weapons saw rapid development in terms of the increase in yield and reduction of weight and size. Thanks to this they could be carried not only by heavy bombers, but also by tactical aircraft and used against tactical targets. Therefore the F-84G introduced aerial refuelling capability and the Low Altitude Bombing System (LABS) with a Mk 7 nuclear bomb. The F-84 Thunderjet was the USAF's last fighter with straight wings. It was succeeded by the F-84F Thunderstreak fighter-bomber, also with nuclear capability, and the RF-84F Thunderflash reconnaissance aircraft, which were also produced in large numbers (3,428) and saw extensive and long service with the USAF and several other NATO nations. The latter type can be considered as the direct predecessor of the F-105.

Even before the F-84F entered service, Republic had commenced work on Advanced Project number 63 – Fighter Bomber Experimental (AP-63-FBX), which was a company-funded development of the RF-84F. The primary mission of the new aircraft was nuclear bomb delivery.

In its initial form the AP-63-FBX was to be powered by the new Allison J71 engine, rated at 14,500 lb (64.5 kN) with afterburner, and to have an internal bomb bay, capable of holding a pair of 1,000 lb (454 kg) bombs or 'special stores' (nuclear weapons), weighing up to 3,400 lb

(1,542 kg). Six 1,000 lb bombs could also be carried on underwing pylons. The defensive armament would consist of four 15.2 mm (.60in) T30 machine guns mounted in the wing roots. The AP-63-FBX was intended to attain a maximum speed in excess of 800 knots (1,480 km/h) at 35,000 ft (10,700 m), to be superior to the rival North American Sabre 45 (F-100 Super Sabre) design.

Before the AP-63-FBX project was proposed to the Air Force, it went through 108 design changes, including the use of two rather than one J71 engines for power, which would have increased the maximum speed to Mach 1.5. By the time the AP-63-FBX was formally proposed to the USAF, the aircraft's length had increased by 10 ft (3.05 m) and the prospective powerplant had been changed to the new Pratt & Whitney J75 two-spool axial flow turbojet engine, rated at 23,000 lb (102 kN) with afterburner, with a variable exhaust nozzle to increase the available thrust. The design would be developed around the YJ75P-3 engine and new MA-8 fire control system. The wingspan was decreased from 36.7 ft (11.18 m) to 35 ft (10.66 m) compared with the original AP-63 design. The 45-degree wing sweep angle was retained, but the new design used the NACA 65A aerofoil section, which was thinner than original F-84F wing. The wings had full span leading-edge flaps, spoilerons on the upper wing surface rather than conventional ailerons, and Fowler flaps on the trailing edge. Flight control would be achieved via an FC-5 Flight Control System developed by General Electric. The air intakes, similar in shape to the straight-across design of the RF-84F, were located in the wing roots. In May 1952 the design was presented to the Air Force Aircraft and Weapons board. The wing was relatively small and had a high wing loading, for stable flight at low altitudes and less drag at supersonic speeds. It did not provide for manoeuvrability or high altitude performance, but this did not matter as the primary mission envisaged for the new aircraft was low-level interdiction and nuclear strike.

The internal bomb bay, although larger than in the original design proposal, could carry less ordnance – a single conventional bomb weighing up to 2,000 lb (907 kg), a single 'special store' weighing up to 3,400 lb or a 350 gallon (1,325 litre) fuel tank.

Pre-mockup set of AP-63-FBX drawings, dated December 1952. Originally the new Republic fighter was to be little more than an enlarged RF-84F with an internal weapons bay. (USAF Museum)

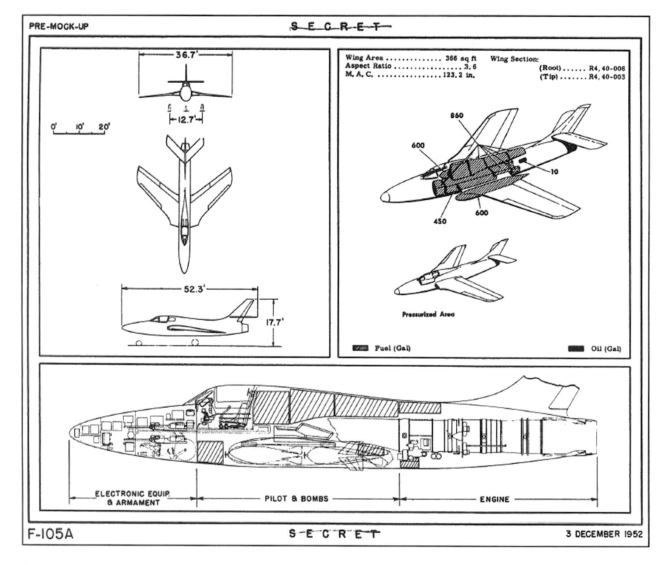

The first YF-105A, (54-0098) on approach to land. (USAF)

The first YF-105A, (54-0098) at Edwards AFB. (USAF)

Under the wings were four hardpoints, with pylons that could carry a single 1,000 lb (454 kg) bomb, two 2,000 lb bombs and drop tanks, or a single 3,000 lb (1,360 kg) bomb. The fifth hardpoint was located on the fuselage underside and could carry up to 2,000 lb of ordnance. The gun armament was changed from four T130 machine guns to a single General Electric T171D (later known as M61 Vulcan) 20 mm six-barrelled rotary cannon with selectable rate of fire of up to 3,000 or 6,000 rounds per minute, with an ammunition drum holding up to 1,028 rounds.

The most important avionics equipment was the new General Electric MA-8 Fire Control System, comprising a modified K-19 sight system, linked to an AN/APG-31 radar ranging system, employing the E-34 radar ranging set, E-30 Toss Bomb Computer and T-145 Special Stores Weapons Release system.

The straight or slab sided fuselage did not incorporate area-ruling with the characteristic 'wasp waist' shaping to reduce the build-up of transonic shockwaves. The tail section design incorporated an 'all-flying' tail, with stabilisers and elevators in the form a single, movable

The first YF-105A, (54-0098), in flight. (USAF)

'slabs'. On the left side in front of the cockpit was a retractable probe for probe-and-drogue in-flight refuelling.

The AP-63-FBX could be used as a conventionally armed fighter-bomber aircraft, but from the outset its primary design mission was that of nuclear strike fighter, considered most vital in the 1950s. It was projected that the aircraft, powered by the J75 engine rated at 23,500 lb of thrust, would attain a maximum speed of 1,230 km/h (664 knots) at an altitude of 35,000 ft, with a combat weight of 28,247 lb, with two underwing fuel tanks and a single nuclear weapon. The service ceiling was to be 33,400 ft (10,180 m) and the combat radius, 959 NM (1,776 km), with the possibility of extending it by in-flight refuelling. As the development of the design progressed, both the manufacturer, Republic, and the customer, the USAF found that these performance figures were inadequate.

Initially, though, the USAF was so enthusiastic about the new nuclear strike fighter, now designated F-105, that in September 1952 they gave Republic a verbal order for 199 aircraft, even though the initial production aircraft were not expected to roll out from the assembly lines until early 1955. In March 1953 this order was reduced by the Weapons Board to a more realistic 46 aircraft – 37 strike fighters and nine reconnaissance aircraft, designated RF-105. In autumn of 1953 the F-105 mock-up was inspected and approved.

By February 1954 the production order was reduced to 15 aircraft and in September of that year it was again cut to just three YF-105 aircraft. In February 1955 the USAF reinstated

the production order for 15 aircraft – two YF-105As (no XF-105 was built), four YF-105Bs, six production F-105Bs and three YRF-105As. It was later changed again to two YF-105As, ten F-105Bs and three RF-105s.

The third YF-105B, (54-0102), at Edwards AFB. (USAF)

The RF-105 was to have a slab-sided nose with KS-24A oblique and vertical camera system and an oblique TV camera with a monitor in the cockpit, replacing the MA-8 Fire Control System and the T-171D cannon with associated ammunition drum. The defensive armament was changed to a pair of M39 20 mm cannons in removable blisters attached to the lower forward fuselage. The RF-105Bs were intended for tactical reconnaissance wings based at Shaw AB, North Carolina, Spangdahlem AB, Germany and Kadena AB, Okinawa. Republic built three RF-105B aircraft, but the programme was cancelled in January 1957 as the McDonnell RF-101 Voodoo was selected for the mission instead. All three airframes (serial numbers 54-0105, 54-0108 and 54-0112) were used by Republic as test and evaluation aircraft, under the designation JF-105, with test equipment installed in the camera bay. These tests included ordnance separation and high-speed control flutter.

The development of the Pratt & Whitney YJ-75 dragged on, so Republic, with the USAF's agreement, decided to install the Pratt & Whitney J57-P-25, rated at 15,000 lb (66.kN) thrust and which also powered the F-100A Super Sabre, in both YF-105A prototypes (54-0098 and 54-0099).

Republic RF-105B (54-0112). Flat panels with camera windows on the sides of the nose are visible. (USAF)

In September 1955 the first YF-105A (54-0098) was completed at the Republic production plant at Farmingdale, Long Island, New York, then dismantled and transported by road to

The third YF-105B, (54-0102) refuelling from the second YF-105A, (54-0099). (USAF)

Edwards Air Force Base, California, where it was first flown by the company's test pilot Russell Roth on October 22. Despite having a less powerful engine than designed, the aircraft managed to exceed the speed of sound easily. The first prototype made 12 more flights, which led to official acceptance by the USAF. On the final flight a main undercarriage strut extended during a 5.5 g turn flown at 530 kts (980 km/h) and was torn off by the airflow. Roth managed to return to Edwards, but the hard landing resulted in major structural damage and the aircraft was scrapped on November 16. The second YF-105A (54-0099), identical to the first one, made its maiden flight on 26 January 1956. However, the results of flight and wind tunnel tests showed that even with the more powerful J75 engine, the F-105 would not be able to attain the intended performance due to excessive drag at high speed.

The third YF-105B, (54-0102) in the company of Kartveli's older jets; the F-84F Thunderstreak, RF-84F Thunderflash and F-84G Thunderjet at Republic Aviation Corporation's airfield in Farmingdale, Long Island. (Republic)

Photograph of the second YF-105B (54-0101) in flight signed by the test pilot Henry 'Hank' Beaird. (Republic)

Prototypes of Century Series aircraft at Edwards AFB. From bottom to top: Lockheed F-104 Starfighter, North American F-100 Super Sabre, Convair F-102 Delta Dagger, McDonnell F-101 Voodoo, Republic F-105 Thunderchief. (USAF)

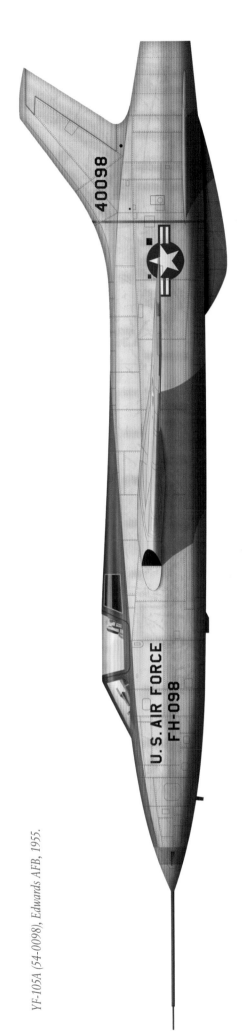

YF-105A (54-0098), Edwards AFB, 1955.

Chapter 2
The first production variant – F-105B

The transition from the prototype YF-105A to the F-105B production version required almost a complete redesign of the aircraft.

The remedy for the disappointing performance was the so-called 'area rule', devised by Richard T. Whitcomb of NACA Langley Aeronautical Laboratory. This involved maintaining a smooth transitions in cross-sectional area along the aircraft's length. This produced a 'wasp waist' shape, narrowing the fuselage where the wings attached, also known as the 'Coke bottle' fuselage profile. Kartveli accepted it, although he found the prescribed profiling excessive and moderated it. The fuselage was lengthened by about 2 ft (61 cm), which gave more room for the radar, and the vertical stabiliser was lengthened by 2 ft and increased in area by over 30% to mitigate directional stability problems at high speed. At its base the fin had an air intake for engine cooling. The ventral fin was also enlarged in area to maintain stability at high angles of attack.

However, this was not the end of the aircraft's problems. The engine installed in the F-105 was not able to push the aircraft into the Mach 1.5 range. The problem was in the air intake design. Another NACA engineer, Antonio Ferri, had developed (originally for the XF-103 interceptor) a forward-swept air intake with a movable plug, adjusting the airflow to the engine requirements through the entire speed range projected for the F-105. This became one of the aircraft's most distinctive features.

This system, known as the variable air inlet (VAI), was controlled by a Bendix Central Air Data Computer and employed a pair of variable 'ramps', which at low and cruise speeds were retracted to allow the maximum amount of air to enter the engine for maximum thrust. At supersonic speeds the ramps moved forward, reducing the cross section of the air inlet to limit the amount of air entering the engine to prevent 'choking' of the airflow through the intake, in conjunction with small doors which opened to bleed off excessive air.

Another distinctive feature added at this stage was the exhaust nozzle divided into four forward-opening segments, known as 'petals', which could be opened in various configurations to act as airbrakes during landing and dive bombing. On landing, only the side 'petals' were opened since the lower one had too small ground clearance and the upper one was in front of the brake chute doors. For dive bombing, all four 'petals' were opened.

The first F-105B-1-RE (54-0100), also known as the YF-105B, featuring all these design changes and, powered by the J75 engine, it made its maiden flight at Edwards AFB on 26 May 1956 with Henry Beaird at the controls. After a successful flight the nose landing gear failed to extend for landing and Beaird made a belly landing on the dry lakebed with minimum damage. Unfortunately the recovery crane operator accidentally dropped the aircraft when loading it onto a trailer, causing more severe damage, resulting in the aircraft being scrapped.

The second F-105B-1-RE (54-0101) also had to perform a wheels-up landing after a test flight because the landing gear failed to extend. It then extended suddenly after the landing. It turned out that auxiliary air intakes located in the main wheel wells, used during ground engine run-ups and taxiing, remained open during the flight, creating suction preventing the wheel well doors from opening. The crash landing, however, broke the suction seal, after which the gear could lower itself.

In 1956 the F-105 officially received the name 'Thunderchief', like the previous Republic combat aircraft with names beginning with 'Thunder'. In 1958 the first 'operational' F-105B (54-0111), the only B-6 variant built, was ready and on 27 May it was accepted by the USAF. The type still had some flaws, but the USAF wanted to work them out themselves.

The performance of the F-105B was impressive for the time, yet with weapons load it was very much reduced. Evaluation in June 1957 showed that supersonic acceleration above Mach 1.8 was still slower than required. The Pratt & Whitney J75-P-5 engine, rated at 23,500 lb (104.5 kN) of thrust with afterburner gave it a maximum speed of Mach 2.08 at 10,700 m

(35,000 ft) in 'clean' configuration, without external stores. The usual combat loading included 4,390 l (1,160 US gal) of fuel in seven fuselage tanks and either two 450 gal (1,703 l) under-wing drop tanks or a single 650 gal (2,460 l) centreline tank. Possible weapon loads were also impressive. The maximum ferry range exceeded 3,057 km (1,650 NM), but with heavy bomb load the combat range was reduced to about 330 km (180 NM). The take-off roll was also very long, which was a feature also quite typical for Republic aircraft, known as 'earth lovers', and which resulted in pilots nicknaming the F-105 'Ultra Hog' (following the F-84 family aircraft being known as 'Hogs').

After the airframe, next to be refined was the all-weather bombing system, known as Weapons System 306A, comprising the General Electric FC-5 flight control system and autopilot, Bendix Central Air Data Computer (CADC) and General Electric MA-8 fire control system, described above. In July 1957, the lightweight AN/APN-105 Doppler navigation system was installed in the F-105 from F-105B-15-RE 57-5785 onwards. Nine earlier aircraft received it as a retrofit. The first fifteen F-105s were used for testing under various climatic conditions, combat evaluation, static-load tests, and tests of the MA-8 fire control system.

The USAF unveiled the F-105B to the public on 28 July 1958, during an air show at Andrews AFB, commemorating 50 years of US Army and Air Force operations. The first fatal accident took place on 16 December 1959, when 54-0106, with Republic chief test pilot Martin J. Signiorelli at the controls, was lost over the Atlantic in unclear circumstances.

A total of 75 F-105B aircraft were built between May 1956 and December 1959: F-105B-5 (five built), B-6 (1), B-10 (9), B-15 (18) and B-20 (38). The B-5, B-6, B-10 and B-15 models were nearly identical. From the fifth aircraft, a change in the cockpit canopy was introduced – small rear view windows, inherited from the RF-84F/AP-63, were deleted and the manually operated canopy with a single hinge point at the upper rear edge gave way to an electrically powered unit with two large hinges at the sides of the fuselage. In Block 20, an arresting hook beneath the rear fuselage was added and the J-75-P-5 engine was replaced by the J75-P-19, which delivered an additional 1,000 lb (4.42 kN) of thrust in afterburner.

The new aircraft were delivered to the 335th Tactical Fighter Squadron, the 'Chiefs', commanded by Lt Col. Robert Scott, at Eglin AFB Test Centre in Florida for Category II operational testing. The testing overran its 30 November 1959 deadline by four months due to technical problems. Project OPTMIZE was introduced to solve technical problems and apply necessary

General arrangement of the F-105B. (USAF)

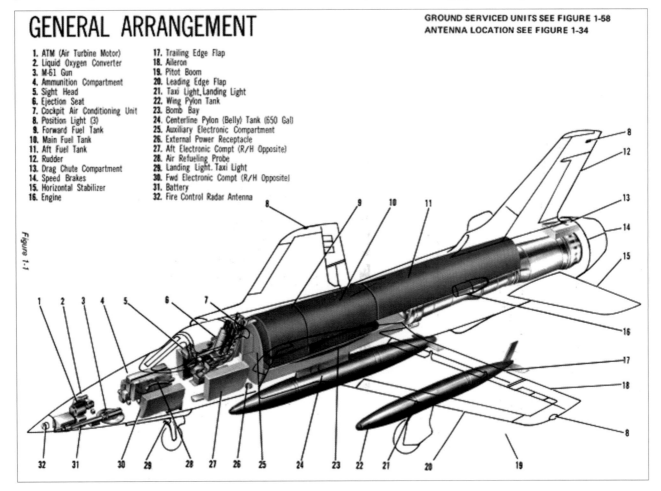

GENERAL ARRANGEMENT

GROUND SERVICED UNITS SEE FIGURE 1-58
ANTENNA LOCATION SEE FIGURE 1-34

1. ATM (Air Turbine Motor)
2. Liquid Oxygen Converter
3. M-61 Gun
4. Ammunition Compartment
5. Sight Head
6. Ejection Seat
7. Cockpit Air Conditioning Unit
8. Position Light (3)
9. Forward Fuel Tank
10. Main Fuel Tank
11. Aft Fuel Tank
12. Rudder
13. Drag Chute Compartment
14. Speed Brakes
15. Horizontal Stabilizer
16. Engine
17. Trailing Edge Flap
18. Aileron
19. Pitot Boom
20. Leading Edge Flap
21. Taxi Light, Landing Light
22. Wing Pylon Tank
23. Bomb Bay
24. Centerline Pylon (Belly) Tank (650 Gal)
25. Auxiliary Electronic Compartment
26. External Power Receptacle
27. Aft Electronic Compt (R/H Opposite)
28. Air Refueling Probe
29. Landing Light. Taxi Light
30. Fwd Electronic Compt (R/H Opposite)
31. Battery
32. Fire Control Radar Antenna

Figure 1-1

The third YF-105B, (54-0102), with mock-up bombs. (USAF)

F-105B weapons suite. (USAF)

Avionic equipment of the F-105B. (USAF)

F-105B assembly line at Republic's Farmingdale plant. (Republic)

modifications to the F-105B, including retrofitting the P-19 engine to older models. On 11 December 1959, Brig. Gen. Joseph H. Moore set a new world speed record of 1,957.73 km/h (average) over a 100 km closed-circuit course under Project Fast Wind at Edwards AFB. Category III test flights began in mid-1960 and were flown by pilots from 334th and 335th TFSs, after these units received new F-105B-10 and B-15 and B-20 aircraft, incorporating the modifications introduced under Project OPTIMIZE. This phase also encompassed weapons testing. The conventional weapons phase was completed by August 1960 at Williams AFB, Arizona. Then the 334th TFS was deployed to Eglin AFB, Florida, to conduct nuclear weapons delivery qualification, which was completed on 15 December 1960. Final testing of all F-105B weapon systems was conducted in 1961 at Nellis AFB, Nevada.

The primary shortcomings of the F-105B were high maintenance requirements, approaching 150 man-hours for each hour of flight, resulting in availability rates dropping below 25%, and a very long take-off run. However, Category II and III trials had shown that it was a stable aircraft with good flight characteristics and accuracy in gunnery and ordnance delivery, yet still lacking the all-weather capability that the USAF wanted.

Republic test pilot Lindell Hendrix in front of the JF-105B (54-0105). (Republic)

The first operational F-105B (54-0111) in low-level flight. (USAF)

A line-up of F-105Bs of the 335th Tactical Fighter Squadron 'Chiefs'. (USAF)

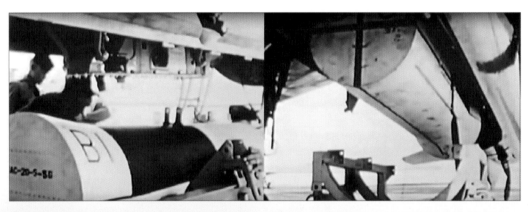

Loading of B28IN nuclear bomb into the bomb bay of an F-105B. (USAF)

Three F-105Bs ready for take-off. (USAF)

The second YF-105B (54-0101) in flight over the Sierra Nevada mountains. (USAF)

Armourers loading 20 mm ammunition belts for the M61 Vulcan cannon. (USAF)

F-105B with full load of Mk-82 bombs. (USAF)

Republic F-105B-20-RE (57-5833) of the 466th Tactical Fighter Squadron, 508th Tactical Fighter Wing, based at Hill AFB, Utah, photographed at Kelly AFB, Texas, in February 1973. (USAF)

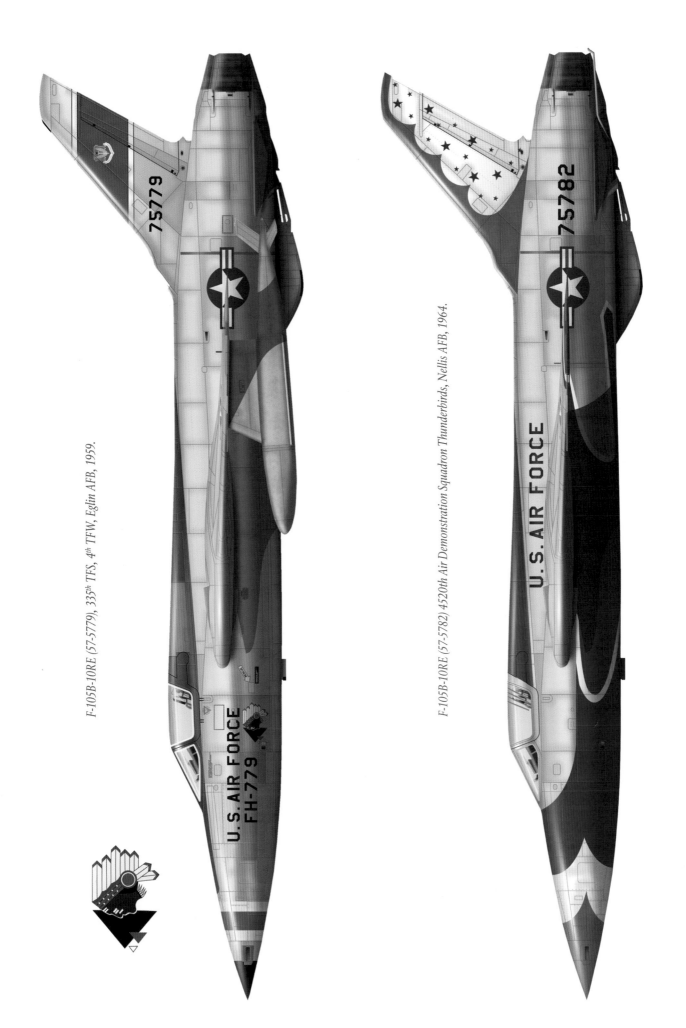

F-105B-10RE (57-5779), 335th TFS, 4th TFW, Eglin AFB, 1959.

F-105B-10RE (57-5782) 4520th Air Demonstration Squadron Thunderbirds, Nellis AFB, 1964.

Chapter 3
The ultimate versions –
F-105D and F-105F

To be a truly effective strike aircraft, the F-105 needed all-weather capability, which in the F-105B was very limited, thus restricting its combat use. To become a true all-weather aircraft the F-105 needed a new electronics and avionics suite, making use of the latest technology. Problems with other systems and the powerplant also needed rectifying. After 75 F-105Bs had been built, the ultimate F-105D variant was developed. The work on this model commenced in 1957.

Republic F-105D-1-RE (58-1146), the first D model built. (USAF)

Lindell Hendrix (left) with the first F-105D-1-RE (58-1146) and a Ford Model T. (Republic)

The most important modification introduced to make the F-105 into an all-weather aircraft was the installation of the AN/ASG-19 Thunderstick navigational and fire control system. This system had an air-to-air and air-to-ground mode allowing automated weapons delivery, both visual and blind, with the use of conventional or nuclear weaponry, including bombs, guided missiles, unguided rockets and internal cannon.

The main component of the ASG-19 system was the NASARR (North American Search and Ranging Radar) R-14A radar, developed by the Autonetics Division of North American Aviation. This radar, operating in the X-band, had air-to-air and air-to-ground attack modes, including ground mapping, contour mapping and terrain avoidance. The radar had antenna of larger diameter, thus requiring a much larger radome than the E-34 ranging radar of the F-105B. The entire nose section was redesigned and the aircraft's length increased from 19.2 m to 19.6 m. The M61 cannon was moved aft and the box-type magazine was replaced by an ammunition drum, using a new feed system with linkless rounds. Another key component of the ASG-19

F-105D assembly line in Republic Farmingdale plant. (Republic)

F-105D-5-RE (59-1750) in flight. (USAF)

Thunderstick FCS was the AN/APN-131 Doppler navigation radar, enabling precise navigation and target finding in every part of the globe.

Two F-105D-15-RE models, 61-0047 and 61-0100 of the 49th TFW. Note open exhaust nozzle petals. (USAF)

In relation to the new avionics suite, the cockpit was redesigned. The most important flight information regarding speed, altitude and vertical velocity was presented on easily read tape bars, which replaced the traditional circular dial instruments of the F-105B.

Another major change was the use of the new J75-P-19W engine, rated at 24,500 lb (109 kN) of thrust with afterburner and 26,500 lb (117.9 kN) for take-off with water injection. The water injection system was to prove invaluable during the Vietnam War, when Thunderchiefs, loaded with bombs and fuel to the extreme, had to take off in the hot and humid climate of Thailand. The rear section of the fuselage was redesigned to accommodate the water injection system and reservoir. The internal geometry and size of the air intake ducting were changed for greater thrust. The extra weight of the additional equipment required stronger landing gear and brakes.

The revised F-105 was approved in March 1958. A programme to equip 14 Tactical Air Command wings with the F-105D was introduced and a production run of 1,500 aircraft was ordered, but this was eventually reduced to the half that number in favour of the McDonnell F-4C Phantom II, which was perceived as a more versatile aircraft.

Three F-105Ds in flight. (USAF)

Formation of four F-105Ds in flight. (USAF)

The first F-105D (58-1146) flew on 9 June 1959 with Lindell Hendrix at the controls. The USAF was still not sure whether the F-105D should be produced or cancelled, so a competition between the F-101 Voodoo and F-105D was conducted, which the F-105D won. The test programme revealed problems with the J75-P19W engine and ASG-19 fire control systems. These were ironed out, though they delayed the Category II tests by more than six months. The Category II tests were conducted by the 335th TFS at Eglin AFB between late December 1960 and 31 October 1961. The F-105D's systems were less troublesome, but the ASG-19 system could still cause problems in hot and humid conditions. During Category II testing, on 10 July 1961 Lt Col. Paul Hoza, commander of the 335th TFS, flew an F-105D non-stop from Eglin to Nellis AFB, Nevada. The 1,520 mile (2,432 km) trip was flown blind all the way at altitudes from 500 ft to 1,000 ft (150 m – 300 m), and included a simulated nuclear bomb delivery and a leg through mountain passes after aerial refuelling over Texas. Category III tests were conducted at Seymour Johnson AFB. Thorough testing was essential due to the vast number of F-105Ds the USAF was planning to purchase at that time.

The testing revealed very good flight characteristics of the F-105D, but the aircraft was very expensive. To reduce costs a USAF board recommended deleting the M61 gun, the ALE-2 chaff dispenser, and the ability to carry ALQ-31 ECM pods, as well as the APS-54 radar warning receiver and the explosive suppression system for the fuel tanks. The board included officers from US Air Force Europe and Pacific Air Force, the primary future operators of the F-105D, but they were outvoted. Fortunately for F-105D pilots the cannon was retained. The deletion of the explosive suppression system for the fuel tanks led several years later to the forced addition self-sealing fuel tanks, a costly modification, in response to combat losses incurred during operations over North Vietnam.

Republic F-105D-10-RE (60-0459) with F-105D-5-RE (58-1159) and RF-101B (59-0458) in the background. (USAF)

In March 1961 the first operational F-105D was delivered to the 4520th Combat Crew Training Wing at Nellis. On 12 May 1961 the first overseas deployment of the type began, when two aircraft were delivered to the 36th TFW based at Bitburg AB, West Germany. In October of that year the 49th TFW based at Spangdahlem, West Germany, received their first F-105Ds. The F-105Ds were manufactured in several production blocks, each differing in some details of equipment. These were: F-105D-1RE, D-5RE, D-6RE, D-10RE, D-15RE, D-20RE, D-25RE, D-30RE and D-31RE. In mid-1962 a major strike at the Republic Aviation production plant curtailed F-105D deliveries and ended only when the federal government invoked the Taft-Hartley Act of 1947, restricting the activity of labour unions.

F-105D firing unguided rockets. (USAF)

Early service revealed several problems with the aircraft and its systems. In spring 1962 two accidents grounded the entire F-105 fleet. European service revealed problems with corrosion and moisture seeping into avionics bays in the F-105Ds with natural metal finish. Thus in June 1962 the USAF embarked on the Project Look Alike modification program to bring standardization to various sub-types within the F-105B and F-105D inventory. With the D, all older variants were brought to the D-25RE standard. All the wiring and hydraulic lines were inspected for signs of chafing and replaced when needed. The equipment bays were opened and resealed and silver lacquer was applied to improve waterproofing and anti-corrosion protection. On this occasion guidance system components for AGM-12 Bullpup missiles were added. The bomb carrying capability was increased to sixteen 750-pound bombs on multiple racks, for a normal nominal load of 6 tons. Actually a 750-pound (340 kg) bomb weighed 823 pounds (373 kg) so

The first F-105F (62-4412) in flight. (USAF)

27

the total bomb load was about 6.6 tons. Older blocks had been fitted only with the refuelling probe, so the receptacle for the flying boom refuelling method was added on the upper nose, ahead of the windshield. This modification proved very valuable during combat operations of the Vietnam, as it enhanced the F-105D's versatility and enabled them to accept fuel from tankers fitted either with the flying boom or hose and drogue, as both types of tankers were used to refuel various USAF aircraft. An arresting hook was added to the tail assembly. Look Alike was a costly and lengthy programme – it took two years and cost $51 million.

The two-seat F-105F

The F-105D with its complex weapon system was a very sophisticated aircraft, and flying it required careful study and monitored transition. A two-seat trainer version with full combat capability was needed for pilot training in flying and ordnance delivery procedures. Previously two twin-seat trainer versions were ordered – the F-105C, a two seat variant of the F-105B, ordered in May 1956 and cancelled in October 1957 in favour of the F-105E, a development of the F-105D. In May 1958 at total of 89 F-105Es were ordered, but in April 1959 this order was also cancelled due to budget restriction in favour of cheaper F-105Ds. However, with F-105D production and deliveries in full swing, the combat trainer was really needed to enable student pilots to achieve proficiency in flying, navigation and bombing techniques to operate the F-105D with maximum efficiency. Therefore, in May 1962 the Secretary of Defence Robert McNamara gave Republic Aviation clearance for development of the two-seat version. The F-105F was an enlarged and heavier version of the F-105D. A 77 cm (31 in) fuselage section was added forward of the wing and two electronics compartments were repositioned. A rear cockpit was added with all controls and instruments identical to the front cockpit. The cockpits were covered by two separate canopies, opening to a 75-degree angle, as opposed to 42 degrees in the F-105D. The vertical fin was increased by 12.5 cm (5 in) in height and also in chord, which gave a 15% increase in area. Since a larger fin produced heavier tail loads, the aft and centre fuselage sections were reinforced. The two-seat version was 1,300 kg (3,000 lb) heavier than

The third production F-105F (62-4414) with test probe on the nose. (USAF) the single-seater, which resulted in the necessity to reinforce the landing gear.

The two-seat version had full combat capabilities, and simulation of combat missions for training purposes and training of pilots in the use of radar and other electronic equipment were its secondary tasks. It could be flown also as single-pilot aircraft, with the rear cockpit

unoccupied, and this happened in Vietnam, where single-pilot F-105Fs sometimes flew in flights with F-105Ds.

F-105F (62-4424) landing with a brake parachute. (USAF)

The first F-105F (62-4412) flew on June 11, 1963 with Carlton B. Ardery Jr at the controls, attaining a speed of Mach 1.15 on its maiden flight. Deliveries of production examples began on December 7,1963. Cost reductions were still required, so it was decided to cancel production of the final 143 F-105D-31RE models in favour of the F-105F two-seaters, which reduced the overall cost of the F-105F purchase by $8 million. The F-105Fs were built in two batches. The first batch of 36 aircraft, with serial numbers 62-4412 through 4447, was completed at the end of the D-31RE production run. The second batch totalled 107 aircraft, with serial numbers 63-8260 through 63-8366. The final F-105F Thunderchief, 63-8366, rolled out of the assembly hall at Farmingdale in December 1964.

Flight characteristics and pilot training

At the time of its introduction, the F-105 was the USAF's most advanced and sophisticated aircraft, so initially only the most experienced tactical aviators, with at least 1,000 hours of total flying time, including 500 hours on other 'century series' types, were selected to fly the Thunderchief. Later, as demand for pilots increased, F-105 training was opened for beginner

The first F-105F (62-4412) in flight. (USAF)

pilots as well. Top graduates of the Undergraduate Pilot Training (UPT) courses were assigned for F-105 qualification. Since the F-105 was at that time the USAF's 'hottest ride', this was the most prestigious and elite assignment. The F-105 pilot training programme, conducted in classes of nine, took nearly nine months and comprised 120 flight hours.

The procedure used to teach student pilots to fly the F-105 was peculiar. The F-105F two-seat version had very limited visibility from the rear cockpit, so the instructor pilot could not take-off and land from that position. Therefore the first three flights were made with the instructor pilot in the front cockpit, who took off and landed, while the student pilot piloted the aircraft in the air, getting the feel of the flight controls and flight characteristics. After three flights with an instructor, the student pilot had his first solo ride, with instructor flying chase in another aeroplane and advising the student pilot on the radio. Thanks to the fact that the F-105 had similar characteristics to the T-38 Talon supersonic jet trainer in which the student pilots qualified before being sent for combat aircraft conversion, and the students were selected from among top UPT graduates, the system worked well.

Flying the F-105

"*It was a great airplane,*" says Michael Cooper, an F-105 pilot. "*Not much of a fighter. But it was so much faster than everything else. The Navy F-4s, we'd fly right through their formations, closing from behind.*"

According to Thunderchief pilot Michael Brazelton, the heavy fighter could make "*860 knots on the deck, well above the speed of sound. Trouble with going so fast so low is that the canopy starts to melt. We had a double canopy, with coolant between the layers.*"

Raw performance aside, the Thunderchief was "*a pretty amazing airplane,*" says Ed Rasimus, who went through a later class at Nellis and served a 100-mission tour with the 421st TFS during May-November 1966. "*We used to do a nuclear profile* [training flight]. *There was a radar mode you could fly at 500 feet. Gear and flaps up, you'd engage the autopilot, set up terrain avoidance, fly 400 miles, deliver a [mock] nuclear weapon on a target, and take the stick back at 200 feet on final.*

"*In training we flew a nuclear profile mission that used all the systems. We would take off and level out at 1,000 feet AGL* [above ground level] *on the altimeter and go 'under the hood'* [The pilot can see the dashboard instruments but cannot see outside as that view is blacked out]. *Engage autopilot and set Doppler nav*[igation] *coordinates to a known point to calibrate the terrain clearance radar for 1,000 feet AGL flight. Then fly a 500-mile round-robin mission under the hood at low level through the Nevada mountains on autopilot using terrain-avoidance radar, altitude hold for the level areas, and Mach hold to climb/descend to keep the radar centreline*

Republic employees in front of the second F-105F (62-4413). (USAF)

F-105 THUNDERCHIEF

LOW LEVEL TOSS BOMBING

⊙ PULL UP POINT
✳ BOMB RELEASE POINT
--- BOMB TRAJECTORY

LOW TOSS

GROUND

HIGH TOSS

GROUND

Nuclear toss bombing methods employed by the F-105.

F-105F (62-4424) with open cockpits. (USAF)

clear of obstacles. Nav was linked from Doppler waypoints to the autopilot and could be updated either by visual or radar.

"At the target, we could deliver a blind offset nuc [lear] shape (that's a radar delivery on a non-returning target up to 10,000 feet offset from a nearby radar image) and the autopilot would do an automatic wings level 4-G (four times normal gravitational stress) pull up to auto-toss the bomb either forward in RLADD (radar low-angle drogue delivery) mode or 'over-the-shoulder' in high toss. The delivery was with an autopilot pull up to weapon release in a 'solution anticipation' mode (the airplane was almost at release parameters when at optimum release angle). The autopilot would then fly the complete Immelman and roll out in altitude hold on a preset heading away from the burst."

Rasimus in a different discussion elaborates on the technique: *"Start four-G pull up straight ahead for about six or seven seconds. Bomb releases in climb at about 30-45 degrees of pitch and flies forward to the target in a ballistic arc. A 'drogue' chute deploys based on a bomb timer to stabilise the bomb and slow descent until a radar ranging mechanism detonates the bomb at a preset height above the ground (air burst rather than the ground burst of the laydown delivery). The delivery aircraft completes a wing-over and escapes about 90-135 degrees off the original run-in course."* [1]

Not all pilots were so enthusiastic. Capt. Anthony Andrews, who flew with the 44th and 34th TFS in 1967 recalls: *"I was an F-104 pilot before being selected for F-105 duty... The F-105 was much larger, heavier, and vastly more complex, but it was designed to be an 800 knot thermonuclear delivery vehicle. Its role as a high speed conventional bomber was, as I saw it, a short-term*

---

1   Posey, Carl, *Thuds, the Ridge, and 100 Missions North,* Air & Space Magazine, February 2009.

An F-105D refuelling in flight by the probe and drogue method. (USAF)

'end-of-life' mission after being replaced by intercontinental missiles. The aircraft was big, heavy and fast, but not necessarily fun to fly. Parts would fall off, a Gatling gun exploded in my airplane one day (a known design problem by General Electric) which tore off a large panel that almost went down the engine intake. We had numerous deformations in the airframes from heavy 'G' force manoeuvring as well. Half of the ejections resulted in broken femurs."

The F-105s might be a nightmare for maintainers, and had their flaws, but many pilots loved their power, speed, and resilience. They could hack their way through the fiercest of defences with heavy bomb load, hit the target, evade the SAMs, escape or shoot down the chasing MiGs and – although not always – bring the pilot back home, often with large bites taken out of them by missiles and flak.

F-105D-6-RE (59-1774) during weapon trials. (USAF)

An F-105D Thunderchief, F-100F Super Sabre and RF-101 Voodoo refuelling from a Boeing KB-50J. (USAF)

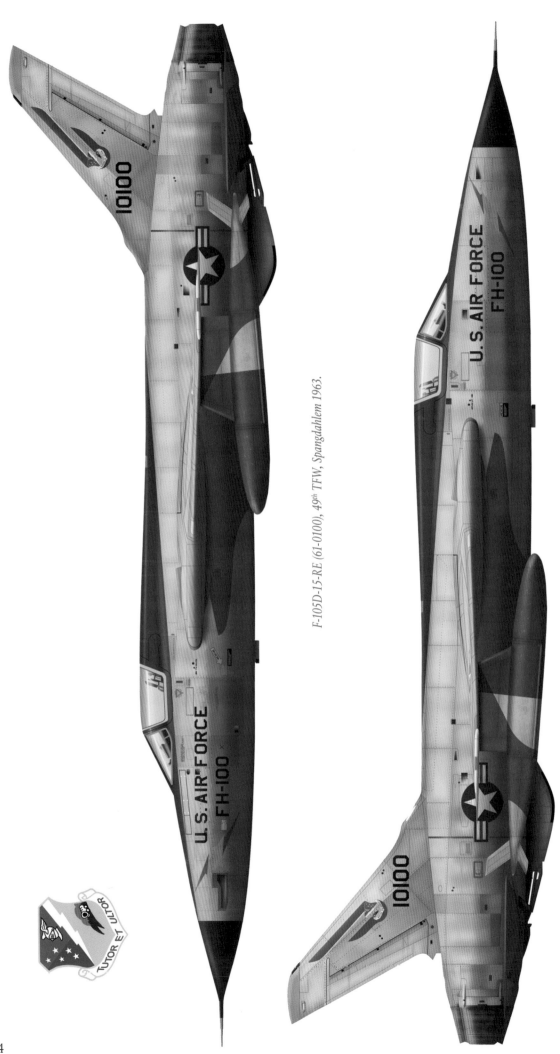

F-105D-15-RE (61-0100), 49ʰ TFW, Spangdahlem 1963.

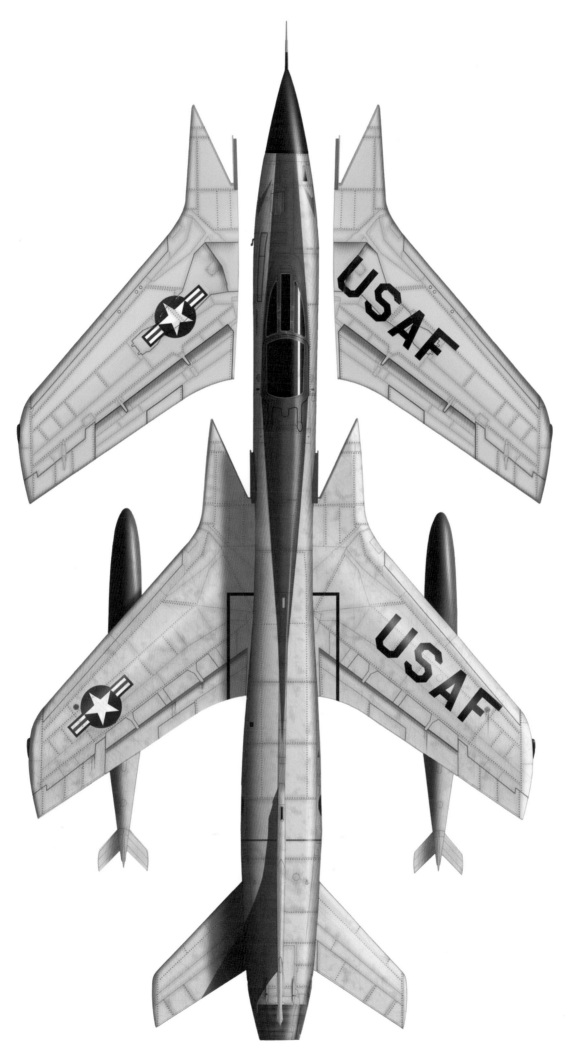

F-105D-15-RE (61-0100), 49th TFW, Spangdahlem 1963.

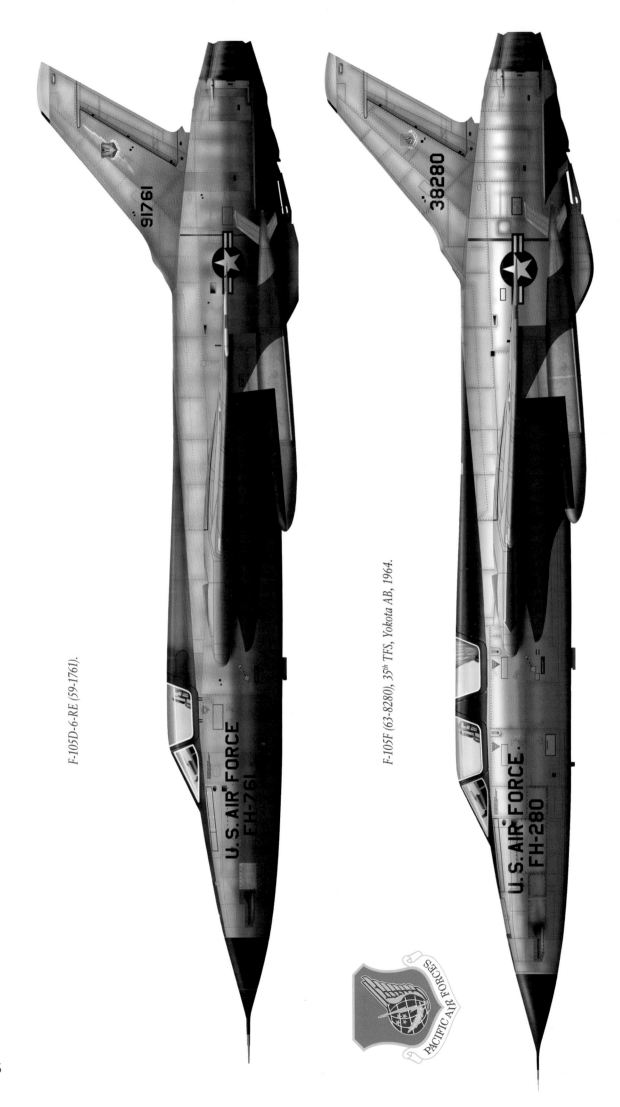

F-105D-6-RE (59-1761).

F-105F (63-8280), 35th TFS, Yokota AB, 1964.

Chapter 4
Wild Weasels and other special versions

Several F-105 versions were developed to meet the requirements that arose in the course of combat operations, particularly from the two-seat F-105F version. These modifications, particularly the best known of them, the Wild Weasel Suppression of Enemy Air Defences (SEAD) variant, extended the aircraft's service life into the 1980s.

F-105F/G Wild Weasel

Complex, integrated and efficient air defence systems posed a major threat to US aircraft operating over North Vietnam. The most potent element of this system was the S-75 *Dvina* (NATO: SA-2 Guideline) surface-to-air missile. The first encounters of American aircraft with these missiles took place on 1 May 1960, when the U-2 spy plane piloted by Gary Powers, flying a reconnaissance mission over the USSR from Pakistan to Norway, was shot down near Sverdlovsk, and on 27 October 1962, when another U-2 piloted by Rudolf Anderson was shot down over Cuba during the Cuban missile crisis. When Operation Rolling Thunder began, the S-75 systems, operated by Soviet crews, were deployed to North Vietnam and quickly began taking a heavy toll on US aircraft. The idea emerged to develop a specialised aircraft equipped with electronic devices to detect signals emitted by enemy radars, which would enable them to be located and destroyed. These aircraft needed crews of two, comprising pilots (known as "nose gunners") and Electronic Warfare Operators (known as "bears"). They would accompany strike missions and suppress enemy air defences.

The first 'Wild Weasel' aircraft were converted F-100F Super Sabres. The F-105F was considered first, but due to the scarcity of these aircraft it was decided to use the slower, but more numerous, F-100F. Seven two-seat Super Sabres were stripped of any unnecessary equipment and fitted with devices adapting them for the mission. The first was the Vector IV Radar Homing and Warning Receiver (RHAW) made by Applied Technologies (later known as APR-25 RHAW). It could scan the S-, C – and X-band frequencies, indicate which type of radar frequency was in use, and direct the pilot onto the radar site. The RHAW had a panel light warning against various types of signals and two 5 in diameter CRT displays in both cockpits, which showed the direction from which the radar signal came, and four antennae – two under the nose, angled at 45 degrees from the aircraft's longitudinal axis, and two atop the vertical stabiliser. Also installed was an IR-133 panoramic crystal receiver, determining the type of radar system being used – a ground control intercept (GCI)

An S-75 Dvina (SA-2 Guideline) surface-to-air missile over Kep air base. (USAF)

F-105F Wild Weasel (63-8311) 'SAM Fighter' from the 354th TFS, 355th TFW. (USAF)

radar, a gun-laying radar or SAM guidance radar. Two antennae were mounted on the fuselage sides and one in the rear. The third major device installed for Wild Weasel missions was the WR-300 launch warning receiver (later known as APR-26 LWR), which detected S-75 missile launches by monitoring the missile guidance frequency. A sudden increase in the signal strength indicated that a launch had occurred.

The F-100F Wild Weasels cooperated with the F-105Ds, locating and marking the missile sites and destroying the radars, initially with 2.75in unguided rockets, and later AGM-45 Shrike anti-radiation missiles, which could be fired at stand-off range and homed passively on emitting radars. The F-100Fs led flights of three F-105Ds, of which one was also armed with unguided rockets or Shrike missiles, and the remaining two with CBU-24 cluster bombs or general purpose bombs, such as the Mk 82, to destroy the missiles, launchers, and command-and-control vans.

Two F-105F Wild Weasels from the 17th WWS, 388th TFW, armed with AGM-45 Shrike anti-radiation missiles on the outboard pylon and AGM-78 Standard on right inboard pylon, en route to target. (USAF)

However, the F-100F/F-105D pairing was less than perfect – the F-100F had no radar, no accurate navigation systems and was considerably slower than the accompanying F-105Ds, which had to zig-zag in order not to overtake the leading Super Sabre.

Due to this problem, the previous decision not to adapt the two-seat F-105F for the air defence suppression role was revisited. The subsequent Wild Weasel II project was based on the F-105F (62-4421) fitted with the AN/APS-107 RHAW, the US Navy's AN/ALQ-51 deception jammer and track breaker, and an external QRC-160-1 jamming pod. This was abandoned in favour of the Wild Weasel III, the F-105F fitted with the same avionics suite as the F-100F

An F-105F from the 333rd TFS, 355th TFW with QRC-160 jamming pod on the right underwing pylon, and ordnance expended. (USAF)

An F-105F Wild Weasel from the 44th TFS, 355th TFW at Takhli in 1970. (Donald Kutyna archive via MLP)

Armourers loading an AGM-45 Shrike missile on an F-105F at Takhli in 1970. (Donald Kutyna archive via MLP)

Wild Weasel. The prototype F-105F (62-4416) was converted by Republic and Sacramento Air Materiel Area to be the testbed of the Wild Weasel III by 3 February 1966, and work to adapt six more F-105F aircraft began. Technical problems occurred with the AN/APR-25 system because of inadequate cabling. All seven aircraft had to be re-worked and re-tested, and conversion of a further six F-105Fs was completed in May 1966. In addition, the ATL AE-100 system was added. This consisted of an array of several small antennas around the F-105F's nose, receiving azimuth and elevation information on Fan Song radar emissions, and a display to indicate the direction of the radar to the pilot. The first five F-105F Wild Weasels arrived at Korat on May 28, 1966. By that time only two of the original seven F-100F Wild Weasels had survived.

In July 1966 a further 18 F-105Fs were converted to Wild Weasels, being fitted with ER-142 receivers, operating in the E-G frequency bands, in lieu of the IR-133. The ER-142 displayed its information on two panoramic cockpit scopes. The F-105Fs were constantly upgraded as the ECM technology and tactics evolved and relevant new devices were developed, so every aircraft had minor differences from the rest. In 1968, the AN/ALR-31 threat detection and evaluation system, with additional wingtip antennas, was installed on several F-105Fs.

The most important enhancement of the F-105F's capability was the provision for carrying the AGM-78A Mod 0 Standard ARM. This weapon, originating from the US Navy's RIM-66

F-105G (63-8320) 'Cooter' armed with AGM-45 Shrike and AGM-78 Standard anti-radiation missiles. (USAF)

F-105G (62-4434) from the 35th TFW. (USAF)

Four CBU-24 cluster bombs, used in attacks on SAM sites. (USAF)

Standard surface-to-surface missile, had a warhead three times larger and range three times longer than the Shrike, thanks to which it could be fired from outside of the effective S-75 missile range. While the Shrike had to be launched virtually directly at the target and could be easily countered by switching off the radar (which broke the targeting lock and caused the missile to go astray), the Standard could make turns of up to 180 degrees, and had a memory circuit to log the last known position of the radar signal and continue towards it.

In September 1967 conversion of 14 F-105Fs to carry the AGM-78 began, and eight of these aircraft entered combat from Takhli in March 1968.

In 1969 the ECM equipment was radically upgraded to handle the AGM-78A Mod 1 and later AGM-78B missiles. The AN/APR-25 RHAW/26 LWR were replaced by the AN/APR-36 and AN/APR-37. The ER-142 was replaced by an AN/APR-35 superheterodyne analysis receiver, installed with the AN/ALT-34 jamming system. A new missile control panel, tape recorder and missile flight tracker were also installed. Deliveries of the "Mod 1" aircraft began in January 1969 and their success in combat convinced the USAF to convert all surviving F-105F Weasels to this standard, re-designating them F-105G. A further 12 F-105F trainers were also converted, which brought the total number of F-105Gs in the inventory to 61. The F-105F Wild Weasels were required to carry ECM devices for self-protection, but the QRC-160-1/8 pods used up one weapons station and could interfere with the SAM detection equipment, so the hardware was split into two fixed pods, housing the QRC-288 and later QRC-335 jammer components,

F-105F (63-8305) during trials with AGM-78 Standard anti-radiation missiles. (USAF)

41

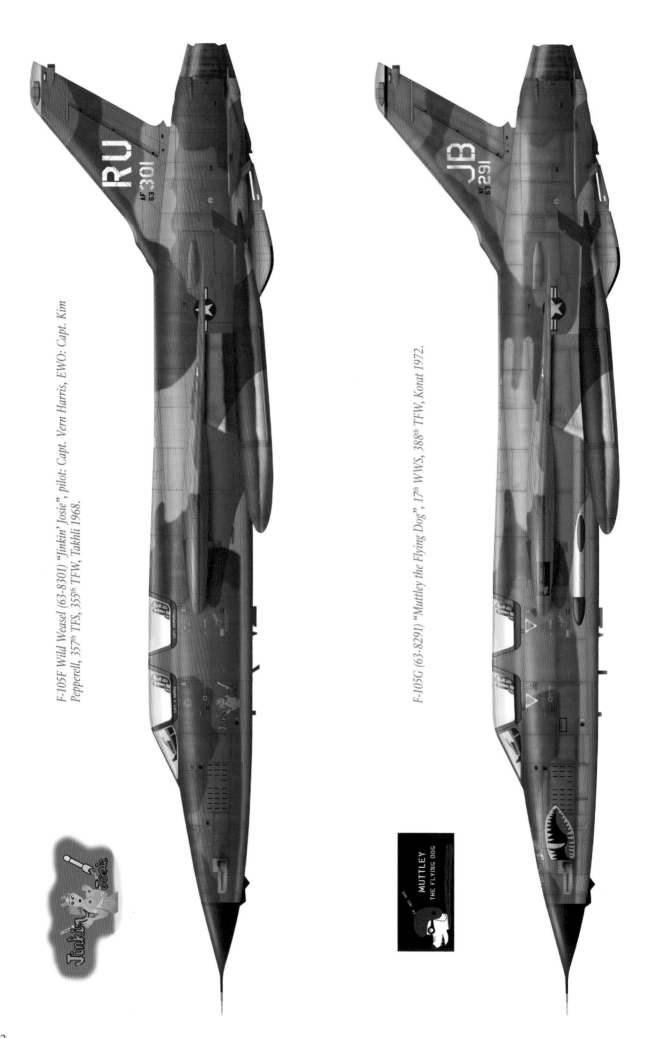

F-105F Wild Weasel (63-8301) "Jinkin' Josie", pilot: Capt. Vern Harris, EWO: Capt. Kim Pepperell, 357th TFS, 355th TFW, Takhli 1968.

F-105G (63-8291) "Muttley the Flying Dog", 17th WWS, 388th TFW, Korat 1972.

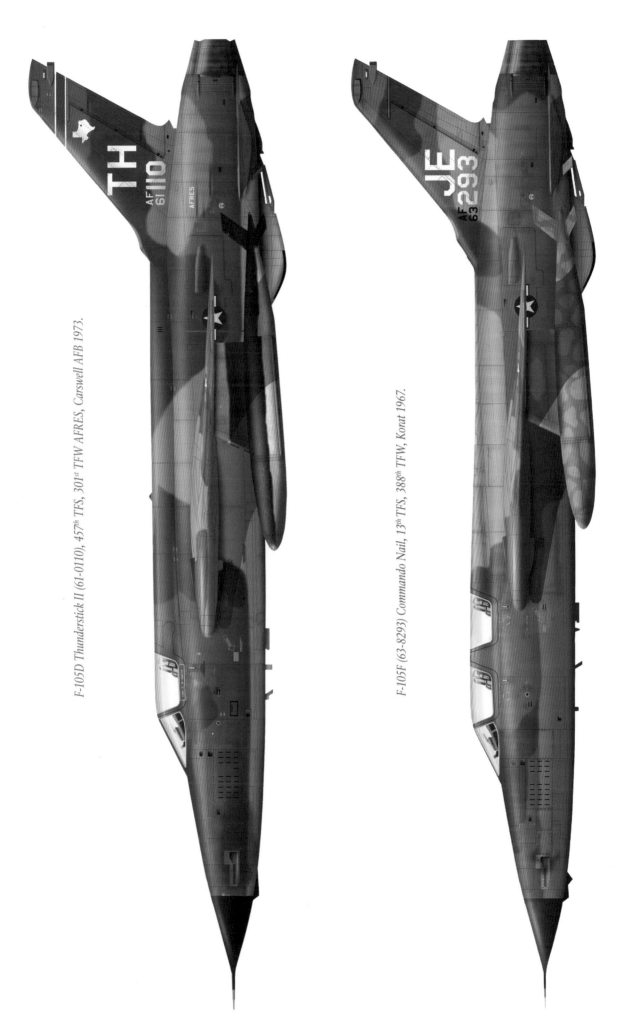

F-105D Thunderstick II (61-0110), 457th TFS, 301st TFW AFRES, Carswell AFB 1973.

F-105F (63-8293) Commando Nail, 13th TFS, 388th TFW, Korat 1967.

attached to each side of the lower fuselage above the bomb bay. As AN/ALQ-105 this system equipped the F-105G variant, and its two elongated blisters are the most distinctive feature of this version, although some entered combat without them and were only retrofitted later.

By the time the bombing of North Vietnam was resumed in 1972 the F-100Ds had been withdrawn from the combat zone and the F-105Gs operated in "hunter-killer" teams with F-4E Phantoms. The F-105Gs located and neutralised the SAM-guidance radars with Shrike and Standard ARMs, and the Phantoms finished the job, destroying the missile sites with cluster and GP bombs.

Combat operations of the F-105F/G Wild Weasels in South East Asia were a challenge. Ground crews struggled hard to keep these sophisticated, essentially experimental, aircraft in airworthy condition. Heat and humidity increased the risk of electronic gear malfunction. The high combat weight put great strain on landing gear, tyres, brakes and brake parachutes.

Commando Nail

In early 1967 the weather really hampered USAF combat operations over North Vietnam. General John D. Ryan, Commander-in-Chief of the Pacific Air Force (CinCPACAF), recognised the problem and was aware that a true night/all-weather strike aircraft was needed to fly bombing missions over North Vietnam on a year-round basis. The entirely new swing-wing General Dynamics F-111A tactical bomber and the F-4E – a new, upgraded version of the Phantom – were still under development. In March 1967, therefore, it was decided to convert a number of two-seat F-105Fs for the night/all-weather radar bombing mission under Operation Northscope, later known as Commando Nail. The four aircraft selected for this conversion had previously been modified to Wild Weasel III standard, with RHAW equipment. In addition,

'Commando Nail' F-105F (63-8269), one of the 'Ryan's Raiders' aircraft. (USAF)

'Commando Nail' F-105F (63-8353). (USAF)

the Commando Nail aircraft had their R-14A radars modified to allow expanded scope picture *F-105G (63-8355) with* and faster sector sweep, which gave the bombardier/navigator (B/N) greater duration of the *bomb bay tank lowered.* radar return, which provided finer target definition on the scope. The pilot's weapon release *(USAF)* switch was wired in parallel to the rear cockpit to allow the B/N to deliver the weapons, and the flight control stick was removed from the rear cockpit. In the front cockpit, a camera was mounted over the radar scope to record target images for bomb damage assessment, but the camera mount limited the forward motion of the control stick and often had to be bent out of the way by the pilot so as not to hamper combat manoeuvring. The paint schemes of the modified aircraft were changed to make them less visible in the night sky, with undersides painted with tan and light green. Since the conversion was General Ryan's idea, the modified aircraft and their crews were called 'Ryan's Raiders'. The following F-105F aircraft were converted to Ryan's Raiders standard: 62-4419, – 4429 (lost on 15 May 1967), 63-8263, – 8269 (lost on 12 May 1967), – 8274, – 8275, 8276, – 8277, – 8278, 8293, – 8312, – 8346 (lost on 4 October 1967) and – 8353.

F-105F Combat Martin

Simultaneously with Commando Nail, another F-105F conversion programme, known as Combat Martin, was developed. This programme had a different objective – the airborne jamming of North Vietnamese communications. At least 13 Wild Weasel III-standard F-105Fs were modified for the Combat Martin mission. The ejection seat in the rear cockpit was removed along with its wiring and hardware, and in its place a Hallifcrafters ORC-128 jamming system was fitted, to block communications between North Vietnamese air defence ground controllers and MiG interceptors. This installation was called 'Colonel Computer' by the crews. A large blade antenna was mounted on the spine, which, along with the seemingly empty rear cockpit, were the external distinguishing features of the Combat Martin airplanes.

The primary mission of Combat Martin aircraft was jamming, but they retained their weapons delivery capability. Once over North Vietnam, the pilot turned the jamming system on and proceeded with the rest of the strike force. Combat Martin aircraft were assigned to both combat wings in Thailand and were operated until early 1970 by the 355th TFW. In November 1970, when the 355th was inactivated, these aircraft were modified to F-105G Wild Weasel standard. One F-105F Combat Martin aircraft, 63-8337, was shot down on 15 April 1968. Among the aircraft converted to the Combat Martin configuration were: 62-4432, 62-4435, 62-4443, 62-4444, 63-8268, 63-8280, 63-8291, 63-8318, 63-8336 and 63-8337.

Front cockpit of an F-105G Wild Weasel. (USAF)

Rear cockpit of an F-105G Wild Weasel. (USAF)

F-105D Thunderstick II

Since the F-105D's introduction into service, the AN/ARN-85 LORAN system had caused severe problems during combat because of its poor reliability. In 1969, thirty F-105Ds were retrofitted with AN/ARN-92 LORAN equipment for more precise navigation. These aircraft were easily distinguished by a long dorsal spine extending from the canopy to the tail fin. This conversion was known as Thunderstick II. With Thunderstick II, a bombing error as small as 50 feet could be obtained from an altitude of 15,000 feet. The first T-Stick aircraft flew on August 9, 1969. They served with the 23rd TFW at McConnell AFB, but were never used in combat. With no LORAN signals over Kansas they were of little use. When the F-105 was transitioned into the Air National Guard/Air Force Reserve, the Thunderstick II F-105Ds were transferred to the 457th TFS of the Air Force Reserve at Carswell AFB in Texas. They stayed there until January of 1980, when they were replaced by F-4Ds.

An F-105D Thunderstick II. Note the extended spine. (USAF)

F-105D Thunderstick II (60-0521). (USAF)

Chapter 5
Operational service

The initial production F-105Bs were delivered to the 335th TFS, 4th TFW based at Eglin AFB in 1958 for Category II testing. The remaining squadrons of the 4th TFW (333rd TFS, 334th TFS and 336th TFS) based at Seymour Johnson AFB, North Carolina began receiving their F-105Bs in 1959. The 4th TFW operated the F-105Bs until 1964, but in June 1960 began replacing them with F-105Ds, again for Category II testing by the 335th TFS at Eglin. The F-105Bs were transferred to the 141st TFS, New Jersey Air National Guard based at McGuire AFB and 466th TFS, US Air Force Reserve (AFRES), based at Hill AFB, Utah. Some went to Nellis AFB, Nevada, to support F-105 pilot training.

Apart from combat units, one more organisation operated the F-105. In 1963 the F-105B was selected for the USAF 4520th Air Demonstration Squadron *Thunderbirds*, as the successor to the F-100C Super Sabre, for the 1964 show season. Nine aircraft were taken from the 4th TFW and adapted for the needs of the air demonstration team. The M61 Vulcan cannon with ammunition supply and MA-8 fire control system were replaced with ballast and two 50 US gal. (200 l) smoke oil tanks, and the bomb bay was converted into a baggage compartment. The aircraft's centre of gravity was deliberately moved aft. The flight controls were upgraded to F-105D standard, and flaps were modified to enable operation at speeds exceeding 500 kt (normally the speed limit for operating flaps was 280 kts). Afterburner light-up time was reduced to two seconds. New radios were added for communication with civilian air traffic control.

The eighth Thunderchief built (54-0107), spent its early career in operational testing and evaluation. It is seen here during cold weather evaluation at Eielson AFB in February 1958. (USAF)

Four aircraft received new vertical fin leading edges made of stainless steel, to withstand the exhaust efflux when flying in the 'slot' position behind and below the leading aircraft and the extra stress involved in the aerobatic manoeuvres. The modified aircraft, serial numbers 57-5782, 57-5787, 57-5790, 57-5793, 57-5797, 57-5798, 57-5801, 57-5802, 57-5814, were delivered between December 1963 and April 1964.

However, the F-105B's career with the *Thunderbirds* was extremely brief and ended badly. On 16 April 1964 the final modified F-105B was delivered, and the team managed to fly only six shows on the Thunderchiefs. On 9 May 1964, during the rehearsal for the show at Hamilton AFB, California, Captain Eugene Devlin, flying No.2 position was attempting to land after a high-speed pass when his F-105B (57-5801) broke apart due to failure of a major structural splice plate on the top of the fuselage, killing the pilot. The F-105 fleet was grounded. Under Project Backbone all remaining F-105Bs were retrofitted with reinforced splice plates. The *Thunderbirds* converted to the F-100D Super Sabre and operated that type until 1969. Some of the remaining *Thunderbird* F-105Bs stayed at Nellis for dart target towing and some had their operational equipment reinstalled. By the end of 1966 they were reassigned to the 141st TFS of New Jersey Air National Guard. In 1967 the 23rd Tactical Fighter Wing at McConnell AFB, Kansas became the Replacement Training Unit for pilots converting to the F-105 and these B models were transferred there from Nellis.

In 1970 the 119th TFS, New Jersey ANG based at Atlantic City Airport, was equipped with the F-105Bs obtained from McConnell, but in October 1972 the 119th TFS was reassigned to the Aerospace Defense Command and began transitioning to the Convair F-106 Delta Dart. The squadron's F-105Bs were transferred to the 141st TFS and 466th TFS US Air Force Reserve (AFRES) based at Hill AFB, Utah. The F-105B remained in service with ANG and AFRES units until 1981.

As mentioned above, the first operational F-105Ds were delivered to 335th TFS in June 1960. In August 1960 the first aircraft were delivered to the 4520th Combat Crew Training Wing at Nellis AFB to enable commencement of pilot conversion. Next were two US Air Force Europe (USAFE) wings, the 36th TFW based at Bitburg AB and 49th TFW based at Spangdahlem AB, West Germany, which received their F-105Ds in May and October 1961 respectively. The remaining squadrons of the 4th TFW, based at Seymour Johnson, began re-equipping with F-105Ds in November 1961. Next TAC unit to re-equip with the F-105D in July 1962 was the 355th TFW, based at George AFB, California. Two wings of the Pacific Air Force (PACAF), the 18th TFW, based at Kadena AB, Okinawa and 8th TFW, based at Itazuke AB, Japan received F-105Ds in October 1962 and May 1963 respectively. The last TAC wing to re-equip with the F-105D in November 1963 was the 388th TFW, based at McConnell AFB.

F-105D-6RE (59-1822) Superhog, 149th TFS, 192nd TFG, Virginia ANG, Byrd Field ANGB, 1980.

The original units equipped with the F-105

Wing	Squadrons	Squadron names	Base	Command
4th TFW	333rd TFS	Lancers	Seymour Johnson, NC	TAC
	334th TFS	Fighting Eagles		
	335th TFS	Chiefs		
	336th TFS	Rocketeers		
8th TFW	35th TFS	Black Panthers	Itazuke, Japan	PACAF
	36th TFS	Flying Fiends		
	80th TFS	Headhunters		
18th TFW	12th TFS		Kadena, Okinawa	PACAF
	44th TFS	Vampires		
	67th TFS	Fighting Cocks		
36th TFW	22nd TFS		Bitburg, West Germany	USAFE
	23rd TFS	Hawks		
	53rd TFS	Tigers		
49th TFW	7th TFS		Spangdahlem, West Germany	USAFE
	8th TFS	Black Sheep		
	9th TFS	Iron Knights		
355th TFW	354th TFS	Fighting Bulldogs	George, CA	TAC
	357th TFS	Dragons		
	421st TFS			
	469th TFS			
388th TFW	560th TFS		McConnell, KS	TAC
	561st TFS			
	562nd TFS			
	563rd TFS			
USAF Advanced Fighter School	4520th ADS	Thunderbirds	Nellis, NV	TAC
4520th CCTW	4523rd CCTS	Hornets		
	4526th CCTS	Cobras		

F-105B-20-RE (57-5807) after a crash landing. (USAF)

F-105F-1-RE (63-8280) of the 35th TFS and F-105D-31-RE (62-4355) of the 80th TFS based at Yokota AB in flight over Honshu island, with Mount Fuji in the background. (USAF)

Newly built aircraft were flown from the Farmingdale factory to the Mobile Air Materiel Area (MOAMA) at Brookley AFB, Alabama, to have modifications installed and from there they were delivered to operational units. The initial phase of F-105 service was plagued by numerous accidents, often resulting in the grounding of the entire fleet. The standard wing strength was approximately 75 aircraft, while in 1960 the 4th TFW had only 60 serviceable F-105B aircraft at any one time. The F-105 had the highest accident rate of any USAF fighter aircraft, reaching 27.5 per 100,000 flight hours in 1964. Apart from Project Look Alike, other modifications were introduced to solve the problems. There were several accidents caused by in-flight engine fires and explosions, so in 1965, under project Safety Pack II, air scoops were installed on the aft section of the fuselage to improve engine bay cooling and venting.

Starting with the 'B' model the F-105 became the USAF's most potent fighter-bomber with its speed, range, ordnance load and avionics. Despite the 'teething problems', immediately upon introducing the F-105s into service the USAF began sending Thunderchiefs on numerous firepower demonstrations and 'show of force' deployments overseas – to Spain, Great Britain, Germany and Okinawa. Later the wing's F-105s operated from Spain and Turkey on NATO alert rotations.

In October 1962 the F-105s nearly went to war, when President John F. Kennedy announced the blockade of Cuba after reconnaissance photos revealed that Russian missiles were being

F-105B (57-5782) of the Thunderbirds demonstration team. (USAF)

shipped to the island and so-called Cuban Missile Crisis began. The 4th TFW deployed their F-105s from Seymour Johnson to McCoy AFB, Florida. At that time the wing had 57 of its F-105s grounded for modifications under Project Look Alike, so the 4520th CCTW from Nellis had to contribute 20 F-105s with pilots and ground crews to the deployment. The wing's air superiority mission was atypical and not suited to the F-105. The deployment lasted until October 29, when the crisis eased.

The primary mission of the two F-105D wings based in Germany was nuclear strike. They stood nuclear alert duty as part of NATO's strategy of massive retaliation during the Cold War period. The squadrons of both wings conducted exercises with other NATO air forces, as they had done previously while operating F-100D fighter-bombers. Simulated weapons deliveries were conducted on Suippes range in France. The F-105D squadrons were regularly deployed from their German bases to the USAF Weapons Center at Wheelus AB, Libya, to practice weapons delivery on El Uotia range in the Sahara desert.

The primary mission of the two PACAF F-105 wings was similar. The squadrons of the 8th TFW were moved from Itazuke to Yokota air base, from where they were rotated to stand on nuclear alert at Osan Air Base, South Korea, since post-war treaties banned nuclear weapons in Japan. The squadrons of 18th TFW based at Kadena AB, on Okinawa, had similar alert duties at their home base. For USAFE F-105 units, the maintenance depot was an Air Force Logistics Command (AFLC) contract facility CASA, Spain's main aircraft manufacturer at Getafe, south of Madrid. European-based F-105s were flown to this facility to undergo major maintenance work and modifications. The maintenance depot for the PACAF F-105 units was also an AFLC contractor Air Asia at Tainan airport, Taiwan.

Two F-105Bs of the Thunderbirds demonstrating 'pistol' formation. (USAF)

A group take-off of the Thunderbirds team. (USAF)

When full American involvement in the Vietnam War began after the Gulf of Tonkin incident in August 1964, F-105 units began to be deployed to a real war. The 'Gulf of Tonkin' resolution commanded the build-up of US forces in South Vietnam and Thailand to conduct retaliatory strikes against Communist forces in Laos and South Vietnam. Immediately after this, the 36th TFS was deployed from Yokota to Korat Royal Thai Air Force Base (RTAFB) in Thailand. It was a prelude to Operation *Rolling Thunder*, an inefficient, almost four-year long, campaign of bombing North Vietnam. On 5 August 1964 the 357th TFS, which had recently moved with the 355th TFW from George to McConnell AFB, was deployed to Yokota to fill in for the Yokota aircraft sent to Korat. During their deployment to Japan, pilots of 357th TFS stood nuclear alert at Osan AB and flew training sorties, but were not allowed to fly combat missions to Laos and North Vietnam.

These deployments in August 1964 started a 16-month period of chaos, when F-105 squadrons from Okinawa and Japan rotated on temporary duty, lasting two to four months,

F-105Bs of the Thunderbirds flying in formation. (USAF)

to Korat and another RTAFB base, Takhli, where the provisional 6235th TFW was formed and squadrons of two Stateside-based TAC wings moved in and out of Okinawa and Japan. In addition to deployments to Asia, squadrons of the 4th TFW took part in numerous exercises and weapons competitions in Florida and Nevada and rotated to Incirlik Air Base in Turkey to stand NATO nuclear alerts.

In 1965 Takhli became the forward base for Yokota, and Korat the forward base for Kadena. The main operating bases provided aircraft, pilots and ground crews and performed scheduled maintenance when the aircraft rotated home.

As the intensity of combat missions was increasing, the USAF command decided to end the turmoil of temporary operation from Thailand and deploy two F-105 wings there on a permanent basis. In November 1965 the 355th TFW was deployed to Takhli and F-105 squadrons began being assigned permanently to Korat, initially under provisional 6234th TFW, replaced by the 388th TFW in April 1966. Operation Rolling Thunder was gaining pace and F-105 losses began to mount. New pilots and aircraft were urgently needed, so the F-105s began to be channelled to Thailand. The squadrons of the 23rd TFW at McConnell AFB assumed the Replacement Training Unit (RTU) role, preparing new pilots to fly the F-105s in combat in SEA. The instructors were pilots who had completed 100-mission combat tours in Vietnam. Initially the squadron of the 4th TFW at Seymour Johnson had a similar role, but the 4th TFW converted to the F-4D Phantom II and transferred its F-105s to McConnell or SEA. By September 1967 both German-based wings had converted to the F-4D and transferred their F-105s to US-based units.

By the start of the Vietnam War the F-105 support depot had been transferred from Brookley AFB to the Sacramento Air Materiel Area (SMAMA) at McClellan AF, California. Rapid Area Maintenance teams from SMAMA, comprising mostly civilian technicians, were also sent to the two Thai F-105 bases to repair combat damage sustained during missions over North Vietnam and Laos. The aircraft that were damaged to a degree

Capt. Eugene Devlin, the Thunderbird pilot killed in the crash of F-105B (57-5801) at Hamilton AFB on 9 May 1964. (USAF)

F-105Bs of New Jersey ANG on the flight line in 1980. (USAF)

Republic F-105B Thunderchief from the 508th Tactical Fighter Group, US Air Force Reserve taking off at Naval Air Station Barbers Point. (DoD)

Three Republic F-105B Thunderchiefs from the 508th Tactical Fighter Group, US Air Force Reserve, and two US Navy McDonnell Douglas TA-4J Skyhawks from Fleet Composite Squadron VC-1 flying in formation off Oahu, Hawaii, on 25 January 1978. (DoD)

F-105D-10-RE (60-0505) in flight over Germany. (USAF)

exceeding the capabilities of the field teams were patched up for a flight to the Air Asia facility on Taiwan or dismantled and shipped there by transport aircraft.

In addition to single-seat F-105Ds, two-seat F-105Fs converted to the suppression of enemy air defence (SEAD) role, known as Wild Weasels, began to arrive in Thailand beginning in May 1966. Later these aircraft also adopted to other roles of night precision strike and electronic warfare (see Chapter 4).

Aircraft operating in SEA constantly received modifications to increase their chances of survival. The primary and secondary hydraulic systems were close to each other, so both were vulnerable to battle damage. A mechanical lock was therefore added to keep the stabilators in the horizontal position in the case of a loss of hydraulic pressure, to maintain level flight instead the leading edge reverting to the up position. Later, a third hydraulic system was retrofitted

F-105D-25-RE (62-4226) firing unguided rockets in a nearly vertical dive. (USAF)

F-105D-15-RE (61-0100) of the 49th TFW in Germany. (USAF)

F-105D-6-RE (59-1762) taking off with a practice bomb dispenser on the centreline pylon. (USAF)

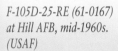

F-105D-25-RE (61-0167) at Hill AFB, mid-1960s. (USAF)

57

Two Germany-based F-105Ds flying in formation with two French Dassault Super Mystères. (USAF)

along the upper fuselage. To provide warning against radar-guided AAA and missiles, an AN/APR-25/26 Radar Homing and Warning (RHAW) system was added, with antenna installed in a fairing under the nose. Aft of the antenna fairing a combat camera was added to record mission results for later analysis. The camera pointed forward when the aircraft was on a dive bombing run and swung aft when the aircraft was recovering after bomb release to record the bomb impact.

In January 1968 a diversion from the Vietnam conflict occurred. On 23rd of that month USS *Pueblo*, a US Navy intelligence ship, was captured by the North Korean Navy. A period of tension began and in response USAF deployed F-105s from Kadena AB to Osan AB, under operation *Combat Fox*. F-105 crews from Korat, Takhli, as well as Nellis and McConnell AFB, were also deployed to Osan to help guard against the crisis, which ended in December 1968 when the crew of USS *Pueblo* was eventually released from North Korean captivity. This incident started a series of F-105 rotations from Kadena AB to Osan, Kwangju and Taegu to bases in Korea, lasting over three years.

On 1 November 1968 President Lyndon B. Johnson halted bombing of North Vietnam under Operation *Rolling Thunder*. Therefore F-105 combat missions from Korat and Takhli were limited to interdiction of Communist supply routes in Laos and South Vietnam and the role of the F-105 began to decline. The type was showing its age and the fleet was decimated by combat attrition and accidents. A week later 388th TFW at Korat began re-equipping its squadrons with a new version of the Phantom, the F-4E, which had more advanced avionics and was more versatile as both air-to-air fighter and strike aircraft, starting with the 469th

F-105D-25-RE (62-4217) refuelling from a Royal Navy Sea Vixen. (Royal Navy)

F-105F (63-8358) at Bitburg. (USAF)

An F-105D on the flightline, early 1960s. (USAF)

TFW, whose aircraft and pilots were distributed among other F-105 squadrons at Korat and Takhli. In May 1969 the 34th TFW followed, leaving the 44th TFW as the only F-105 squadron at Korat. In October this squadron was transferred to the 355th TFW at Takhli, which became the only base in SEA operating Thunderchiefs.

Diminishing demand for F-105 pilots resulted also in reduction of the number of Replacement Training Units. Three of four squadrons of the 23rd TFW at McConnell reverted to combat unit status. The first to do so was the 561st TFS, which became a Wild Weasel Squadron, flying F-105Gs. Next was the 562nd TFS. Most of the thirteen graduates of its last RTU class in August 1970 were assigned to McConnell rather than Thai-based squadrons. By August 1970 the 419th TFW remained the only F-105 training unit at McConnell. Its last class of eight graduated in May 1970 and the squadron deactivated in May 1971. In 1970 the 563rd TFS received modified F-105D Thunderstick II aircraft (see chapter 4).

The 355th TFW flew the last F-105 combat missions in October 1970, and shortly thereafter the wing's 48 F-105s were flown back to McConnell, the only stateside USAF base still operating this type. Most were put into flyable storage, awaiting overhauls and delivery to AFRES and ANG squadrons scheduled to receive them. In December 1970 the 355th TFW was deactivated and the Takhli base was shut down. The only F-105s left in SEA were the Wild Weasels, gathered previously at Korat. They were initially assigned to Detachment 1 of the 12th TFS,

Republic F-105D-31-RE Thunderchief (62-4386) from the 563rd TFS at Yokota AB. (USAF)

An F-105D of the USAF Fighter Weapons School flying in formation with an F-100D Super Sabre and RF-4C Phantom. (USAF)

An F-105D at Osan AB, South Korea, during the Pueblo crisis in 1968. (USAF)

F-105Ds and one F-105F of the Air Force Reserve 465th Tactical Fighter Squadron, 507th Tactical Fighter Group (later 301st TFW), on the flight line at Tinker AFB, Oklahoma, June 1978. (DoD)

A pilot climbing into the cockpit of an F-105D. (USAF)

F-105F (63-8328) of 561st TFS, 23rd TFW on approach to landing after a training flight. (Donald Kutyna)

An F-105F being serviced at Bitburg AB circa 1966. Note the practice Mk 28IN thermonuclear bomb on the bomb loader under the open bomb bay. (USAF)

Armourers loading a practice B43 thermonuclear bomb into the bomb bay of an F-105D. (USAF)

subordinated to the 18th TFW at Kadena, but on 1 November 1970 this unit was absorbed by newly-formed 6010th Wild Weasel Squadron (WWS), which was assigned to the 388th TFW. In 1971 this squadron was renamed 17th WWS.

The remaining USAF units operating the F-105s were the 18th TFW at Kadena, 23rd TFW at McConnell and 57th Fighter Weapons Wing at Nellis. Of the original 833 F-105s only 264 were still flying, including 45 F-105Bs, operated by two ANG squadrons. Only for the F-105G Wild Weasels there were no replacements, the remaining former F-105 units were being equipped with either F-4s or A-7Ds. The surviving Thunderchiefs were transferred to Air National Guard units. The first ANG unit to receive them was 184th Tactical Fighter Group based at McConnell, which took over the role of F-105 training unit from 23rd TFW, becoming the 184th Tactical

F-105Ds of the Air Force Reserve 465th Tactical Fighter Squadron, 507th Tactical Fighter Group after arrival at Tinker AFB, Oklahoma in May 1972. (USAF)

*F-105D-6-RE (59-1760) from the 121st TFS, District of Columbia
ANG. (USAF)*

An F-105F landing at sunset. (USAF)

***Above:** F-105F (63-8307)
of the USAF Fighter
Weapons School in flight
over Nevada. (USAF)*

*An F-105F landing with
empty MER. (USAF)*

F-105D-10-RE (60-0496) from the 121st TFS, District of Columbia ANG. (USAF)

Crew chief preparing an F-105D for a training mission. (USAF)

F-105D-31-RE (62-4383) of the US Air Force Reserve 465th Tactical Fighter Squadron, 507th Tactical Fighter Group, after landing at RAF Mildenhall, June 1978. (DoD)

An F-105G from the 128th TFS, Georgia ANG with two practice Mk 82 bombs on the centreline MER and two practice AGM-45 Shrike missiles on outboard underwing pylons. (DoD)

Fighter Training Group. In January 1971 the 149th TFS of Virginia ANG, based at Byrd Field, Richmond, received its F-105s. In April 1971 the 121st TFS of District of Columbia ANG, based at Andrews AFB, Maryland, converted to the F-105D.

The next to receive the F-105Ds and Fs were three US Air Force Reserve (AFRES) squadrons. In May 1972 the 465th TFS 'Sooners', based at Tinker AFB, Oklahoma, received F-105s from Kadena. The 23rd TFW was relocated from McConnell to England AFB, Lousiana, and converted to the A-7D, handing over thirty F-105D T-Stick IIs to AFRES 457th TFS based at Carswell AFB, Texas. In September 1972 several D and F models were transferred to the 466th TFS AFRES based at Hill AFB, Utah. This squadron was the last unit operating the F-105, which it did until February 1984.

An F-105 pilot of the 128th TFS, Georgia ANG. (DoD)

F-105G (63-8285) of Georgia ANG with a rocket launcher on centreline MER and practice AGM-45 Shrike missiles on outboard underwing pylons. (USAF)

Three F-105Fs from the 561st TFS, 23rd TFW in flight with SUU-21 practice bomb dispensers. (Donald Kutyna archive via MLP)

In April 1972 President Richard M. Nixon resumed bombing of North Vietnam, attempting to stop the North Vietnamese offensive in South Vietnam. On 12 April 12 F-105G Wild Weasels from the 561st TFS were deployed from McConnell to Korat as 'Detachment Alpha' under Operation *Constant Guard I*, joining other F-105Gs of the 17th WWS during bombing campaigns over North Vietnam, Laos and Cambodia, codenamed *Freedom Train*, *Linebacker I* and *Linebacker II*. Meanwhile the home base of the 561st TFS was relocated from McConnell to 35th TFW at George AFB, California.

Combat operations of the F-105 Wild Weasels in SEA ended in April 1973. The crews of Detachment Alpha returned to George AFB, leaving their 12 F-105Gs at Korat, where they

stayed under the care of one pilot and 180 ground crews until September, when they were ferried to George AFB.

In October 1974 the last F-105Gs of the 17th WWS at returned to George AFB and were assigned to the reactivated 562nd TFS. The 35th TFW was the last active duty unit operating the F-105s.

The last F-105G (63-8299) from the 128th TFS, Georgia ANG. (USAF)

Starting in July 1973 the ANG and AFRES units began transferring their F-105s to the 'Boneyard' – Military Aircraft Storage and Disposition Centers (MASDC) at Davis-Monthan AFB, Arizona (later renamed Aerospace Maintenance and Regeneration Center – AMARC and Aerospace Maintenance and Regeneration Group – AMARG). By 1983 a total of 94 F-105s were delivered there.

After the return from war, F-105 operations remained those of the pre-war era, but were far less intense. In 1976 F-105s began participating in a series of European deployments, code-named *Coronet*. The last was *Coronet Rudder* in August 1981, to Denmark.

The 35th TFW was the last active duty USAF unit operating the F-105G Wild Weasels. In October 1978 the wing began transferring them to the 128th TFS of Georgia ANG at Dobbins AFB. The conversion was completed on 12 July 1980, when the 562nd TFS hosted a 'Sawadee' (Thai farewell) party, celebrating the retirement of the F-105 from active USAF service.

The 128th TFS operated F-105Gs until May 1983, when they flew the last 15 planes to Naval Air Station Patuxent River, Maryland. From there they were transported by barges up Chesapeake Bay to US Army Aberdeen Proving Ground, where they were used as targets for missile tests, a bitterly ironic end for aircraft intended for destroying missile sites.

The last unit operating the F-105 was the AFRES 419th TFW, based at Hill AFB. In June 1983 the unit flew the final F-105 mission, comprising 24 planes (the 25th aborted on the ground) that made a flypast over the base and flight to the bombing range. Flying in the rear cockpit of one of the F-105Fs was retired Col. Leo Thorsness, the most notable Wild Weasel pilot, who was awarded the Medal of Honor for a mission over North Vietnam on 19 April 1967 and was shot down a few days later and spent nearly six years in North Vietnamese captivity.

On 25 February 1984 a final 'Thud Out' ceremonial flight and party was hosted by the 419th TFW at Hill AFB. By that time 612 of the original 833 F-105 aircraft had been lost in combat and accidents or scrapped.

After retirement the surviving F-105s met various fates. Many were scrapped, some were used as targets for weapons at Aberdeen and Soccoro, New Mexico, where they were used for testing the results of projectile hits on airframes. After these tests the wrecks of the planes were sold as scrap metal. Several examples were used for Aircraft Battle Damage Repair training and eventually also sold for scrap. Ten aircraft were delivered to the 343rd Training Squadron at Lackland AFB, San Antonio, Texas to teach USAF Security Police recruits how to guard parked airplanes. Some found their way to various museums or ended as gate guardians at air bases.

Chapter 6
F-105 in combat over Vietnam

On 2 August 1964 the American destroyer USS *Maddox*, conducting a signals intelligence patrol in the Gulf of Tonkin, was attacked in international waters by North Vietnamese torpedo boats. This so-called "Gulf of Tonkin Incident" marked the beginning of the Vietnam War as an open conflict between the USA and North Vietnam. US Navy warplanes conducted retaliatory strikes on targets on the North Vietnamese coast. On 7 August the Congress passed the Gulf of Tonkin Resolution, empowering President Lyndon B. Johnson to use conventional forces in South-East Asia. Bomber squadrons equipped with the Martin B-57 Canberra and fighter squadrons with the Convair F-102 Delta Dagger and North American F-100 Super Sabre were deployed to Bien Hoa and Da Nang bases in South Vietnam. On 12 August 18 F-105Ds of the 36th Tactical Fighter Squadron from Yokota AB, commanded by Lt Col. Don McCance, were secretly deployed to Korat RTAFB in Thailand. It was not the first F-105 deployment to Korat – in April 1964 F-105Ds from the 44th TFS were deployed there for exercise Air Boon Choo, which involved testing the feasibility of operating the F-105 from a jungle air base.

Operations of the US and South Vietnamese air forces against Viet Cong supply routes leading from North to South Vietnam in Laos soon began. The first F-105 combat operation was a Rescue Combat Air Patrol (RESCAP) mission for the crew of a T-28 Trojan of Air America (the dummy airline operated by the US Government as a cover for covert operations), shot down over the Plain of Jars in Laos on 14 August. During this mission F-105D (62-4371), flown by 1stLt David Graben, was hit by enemy fire when strafing an AAA site, but managed to return to Korat, although the aircraft was damaged beyond repair. This situation, which became typical during many later missions, demonstrated the toughness of the Thunderchief despite the vulnerability of its hydraulic system.

These US actions resulted in an increase of material support for North Vietnam from the Soviet Union and China. General Hunter Harris, commanding the Pacific Air Force, wanted every such increase in North Vietnam's war potential to be neutralised by US counter strikes, but President Johnson, listening to civilian advisors rather than military commanders, refused. Instead, he allowed only limited, gradually escalating responses to specific North Vietnamese threats, in order to attempt to dissuade its communist leaders from attempting to unify Vietnam under their rule.

An F-105D readied for a combat mission at Korat RTAFB early in Operation Rolling Thunder, *spring 1965. (USAF)*

On 1 November 1964 the Viet Cong infiltrated Bien Hoa Air Base, destroying ten US aircraft and killing four airmen. The commanders of US services immediately requested a retaliatory strike on Noi Bai airfield, where the North Vietnamese 921st Fighter Regiment was being formed, but President Johnson, running for re-election, refused, allowing only an intensification of strikes on the Ho Chi Minh trail in Laos. Johnson rejected the proposal to destroy the most important parts of North Vietnam's infrastructure, such as bridges, railway lines and airfields. Instead he chose a gradual intensification of attacks, beginning with a month-long bombing campaign against targets in Laos, conducted primarily by the Republic of Vietnam Air Force, moving gradually into the territory of North Vietnam over the next six months. This tactic was intended to demonstrate the combat potential of US air power to North Vietnamese leaders, in the hope of discouraging them from interfering in the affairs of South Vietnam, and test the reaction of USSR and China. It failed entirely: the leaders and people of North Vietnam united in their resistance, and slow escalation allowed the North Vietnamese to develop a very elaborate and effective air defence system with Soviet and Chinese support.

F-105Ds on the flightline at Takhli RTAFB in 1965. (USAF)

On 15 December 1964 the F-105Ds began attacks on targets in Laos under Operation Barrel Roll, which commenced on 10 December. These were attacks on supply routes, conducted by formations consisting of up to four aircraft. For the F-105Ds and their pilots, which mainly specialised in nuclear weapons delivery, these were new and difficult tasks. During nuclear weapons delivery, flown on autopilot coupled with the Toss Bomb Computer, the pilot did not need to see the target and relatively little precision was required. Combat operations over Laos consisted of precise, synchronised formation attacks on small, well-camouflaged, often mobile targets from low altitude, after previous identification, often in poor visibility, yet without the assistance of Forward Air Control aircraft. The F-105Ds also flew escort missions for RF-101 reconnaissance aircraft.

In February 1965, in response to Viet Cong attacks on US bases in South Vietnam the US and South Vietnamese air arms conducted Operation 'Flaming Dart' – attacks on North

Vietnamese Army bases in North Vietnam and Viet Cong bases in South Vietnam. On 3 March 1965 Operation *Rolling Thunder* began. It was a 44-month long, ultimately ineffective, bombing campaign against North Vietnam, in which the F-105s bore the brunt of the attacks and suffered extremely heavy losses due to AAA guns, surface-to-air missiles, fighters and accidents.

Targets for the F-105s were usually military storage depots, railway yards, bridges, and from mid-1966, POL (petroleum, oil and lubricant) storage sites, supply dumps, barracks and industrial targets, such as the Thai Nguyen steel plant or power plants. The USAF often had poor intelligence data and the targets were often referred to as 'suspected', which sometimes meant that they were non-existent and the pilots simply dropped bombs on the jungle. From mid-1966 on the bombing campaign intensified with increasing number of raids on targets in 'Route Package 6' (see below). Mounting losses due to increasing MiG activity resulted in clearance for attacks on North Vietnamese airfields on 23 April 1967. Thanks to this, several NVAF fighters were destroyed on the ground at Kep and Hoa Lac air bases. In addition to these raids, interdiction and armed reconnaissance missions to hamper the flow of war materials in lower Route Packages and Laos were flown. These missions, consisting of attacks on road intersections, fords, etc., were usually of marginal effectiveness and apart from 'moving the dirt around' did not achieve anything to interrupt the flow of supplies for the Communist forces.

The intensity of operations was high. When the weather allowed, both F-105 wings had to put up 4-5 flights of four aircraft (plus the fifth as spare in case of a failure or abort of one of the aircraft of the main package) for two combat missions, in the morning and afternoon. Additionally a Quick Reaction Alert flight, scrambled in the event of an emergency, stood in readiness. With such intensity of operations in the hot and humid climate of Thailand, keeping the sophisticated F-105s in airworthy condition required enormous, constant effort by the maintenance crews. After several crashes caused by engine failures it was decided to significantly shorten the Time Between Overhauls of the engines, as merciless exploitation at full military power and heavy use of afterburners in combat conditions caused their rapid wear.

An F-105D approaching a KC-135 tanker with refuelling probe extended, en route to the target in North Vietnam in 1965. (USAF)

Republic F-105D-25-RE Thunderchief (61-0217) of the 67th TFS. On 16 September 1965 the squadron commander, Lt Col. Robinson Risner, was flying this aircraft when he was shot down by anti-aircraft artillery. (USAF)

Captains Benjamin Bowthorpe (left) and Donald Totten from the 334th Tactical Fighter Squadron, 355th TFW, were the first F-105 pilots to complete 100 missions over North Vietnam, on 11 January 1966. (USAF)

The Route Package system

In the initial months of Operation Rolling Thunder the US Air Force, operating from bases in South Vietnam and Thailand, and US Navy, operating from aircraft carriers in the Gulf of Tonkin, had difficulties in conducting joint operations. Both services found themselves competing for resources and targets, so in December 1965 the territory of North Vietnam was divided into six sectors, known as 'Route Packages', in order to separate operations of each service. Route Package 1 referred to the southernmost 'panhandle' part of North Vietnam, near the Demilitarised Zone. Route Packages 2, 3 and 4 referred to the central part of the country, Route Package 5 referred to the north-western part and Route Package 6, the north-eastern part, encompassing the Red River Delta with the capital Hanoi and the main port of Haiphong (through which most supplies, delivered from the Soviet Union, China and other communist countries, went). Route Packages 2, 3 and 4 were assigned to the US Navy as they bordered the Gulf of Tonkin. Route Packages 1, 5 and 6 were assigned to the USAF. In April 1966 'Route Package 6' was divided into two sections, inland 6A with Hanoi, assigned to the USAF and coastal 6B with Haiphong, assigned to the US Navy. The most important targets were located within RP 6, which was described as the most heavily defended airspace in the world due to the huge concentration of radar-guided AAA batteries, surface-to-air missile sites and fighters.

Therefore the F-105 pilots coined the term 'going downtown' for missions to RP 6, after Petula Clark's hit 'Downtown' of 1965, which included the lyrics "*downtown everything is waiting for you*". The most prominent terrain feature of RP 6 was the 24-km long and 1,500 m (5,000 ft) high Tam Dao mountain range, pointing from the north-west towards Hanoi, which became known as Thud Ridge. It was used as a landmark and terrain-masking feature by Thunderchief formations inbound for targets around Hanoi and was littered with jettisoned fuel tanks and weapons pylons, as well as F-105 wreckage. RP 1 was deemed the safest, since there were no crucial targets there and it was closest to Thailand. The closer a Route Package was to the Laotian border, the greater the probability of rescue for the pilot by Combat SAR teams.

Thanh Hoa bridge raids

Some of the most remarkable and disastrous missions of the Rolling Thunder campaign were the attacks on Ham Rong ('Dragon's Jaw' in Vietnamese) bridge near the village of Thanh Hoa, 120 km (75 miles) south of Hanoi. It was a vital railway and road bridge over the Song Ma river. It was quite short (160 m, 540 ft) and of very strong construction – twin steel through-truss spans set on nine concrete piers. The North Vietnamese realised the importance of the bridge and set a vast network of AAA guns around it.

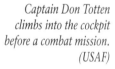

Captain Don Totten climbs into the cockpit before a combat mission. (USAF)

F-105D-20-RE (61-0127) refuelling from a KC-135 en route to a target in North Vietnam in 1965. At this early stage of the war the aircraft had no camouflage. (USAF)

Early in the Rolling Thunder campaign a decision to interdict the North Vietnamese railway network was made. On 3 April 1965 Rolling Thunder Mission 9-Alpha was flown against the Thanh Hoa bridge. The bridge was a difficult target and the mission result was to reflect this.

The strike force, commanded by Lt Col. Robinson Risner, a Korean War ace with eight victories to his credit and commander of the 67th TFS, consisted of 79 aircraft, including 46 F-105 Thunderchiefs of the 67th TFS from Korat and 354th TFS from Takhli as the main strike force, 21 F-100 Super Sabres to provide AAA suppression and fighter escort, two RF-101C Voodoos to conduct damage assessment, plus ten KC-135 tankers. Sixteen of the F-105s were armed with two AGM-12 Bullpup command-guided missiles and the remaining thirty were armed with 750-lb M117 bombs. The Bullpups were fired one at a time, so two passes of each aircraft were required.

The precisely coordinated attack began at 1400 hours, with Risner in the leading aircraft. The 32 Bullpups, launched at about 12,000 feet, proved difficult to guide, and those that did hit the target did not inflict significant damage. Their warheads were too light and they simply bounced off the structure. The effect of the 120 M117 bombs that hit the bridge was

F-105D-25-RE (61-0163) from the 562nd TFS deployed from McConnell AFB to Thailand, en route to the target in North Vietnam in 1965. (USAF)

The map of North Vietnam with Route Package division. (USAF) Ingress and egress routes of US warplanes in North Vietnam. (USAF)

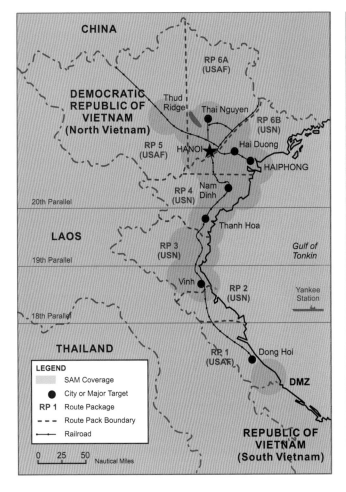

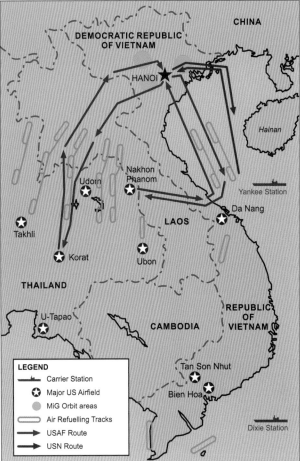

An F-105D carrying napalm canisters. (USAF)

A flight of four F-105Ds refuelling en route to the target in North Vietnam in 1966. Early in the war, not all F-105s deployed to SEA were camouflaged. (USAF)

also negligible. One F-100 and one RF-101 were shot down and Risner's aircraft was severely damaged, forcing him to land at Da Nang in South Vietnam.

Another strike was ordered the following day. This time all 48 F-105Ds were armed with M117 bombs. They were supported by 21 F-100 Super Sabres. The strike force was again led by Risner. However, his precise attack plan was thwarted by the weather. The strike force was divided into flights of four, which attacked the target at intervals, allowing each flight to drop bombs and clear the target area for the next one.

Risner attacked first. He made a dive bombing pass and after the bomb release he climbed for altitude and began circling over the target, directing the subsequent strikes. His wingman, Capt. Carlyle Harris, was hit by flak coming off the target. Harris ejected and became a PoW for nearly eight years.

Delays of the tankers meant that several flights had to orbit in the vicinity of the target, waiting for their turn for attack. The Zinc flight from the 354th TFS flight was jumped by four MiG-17 fighters from the 921st Fighter Regiment, based at Noi Bai. Zinc Lead, Maj. Frank Bennett and Zinc 02, Capt. James Magnusson, were shot down and killed. One of the MiGs was shot down by Capt. Don Kilgus of the 416th TFS. It was the only F-100D air-to-air victory of the war, yet unconfirmed. The bridge was damaged, but not knocked down. It was not destroyed until 1972, requiring several attacks by USAF and US Navy aircraft, armed with laser-guided bombs and TV-guided Walleye bombs.

The disastrous raids on Thanh Hoa bridge were an important lesson for the USAF for three reasons. Firstly, they proved that M117 bombs and Bullpup missiles were useless against really hard targets – to destroy them, heavier weapons were needed. The F-105s could haul a heavy

bomb load, but externally carried bombs and fuel tanks degraded their range, speed and agility. Therefore a compromise had to be found between required performance and weapons load, leading to the introduction of rather small loads, comprising usually 6-7 bombs. The compromise was also good for other reason – in the event of a MiG attack all ordnance was immediately jettisoned, so carrying smaller loads meant wasting fewer bombs, which were in short supply. The raid also influenced the composition of later strike packages. It marked also the introduction of 'hit and run' tactics by the North Vietnamese fighter force. To increase protection against such attacks the USAF introduced Lockheed EC-121 Warning Star airborne early warning aircraft, codenamed 'Disco', orbiting over the Gulf of Tonkin. Their radars covered North Vietnamese, Laotian and part of Chinese airspace. However, as Ed Rasimus recalled, their warnings were often imprecise and belated, causing additional confusion among combat aircrews over North Vietnam.

Paul Doumer bridge raids

The most successful mission flown by F-105s during Operation Rolling Thunder was the Paul Doumer bridge raid. The Paul Doumer (Vietnamese: Long Bien) bridge, 2,570 m (8437 ft) long and 11.6 m (38 ft) wide, built by the French during 1899–1902, was the only railway crossing over the Red River. It linked Hanoi with the port of

An USAF pilot in front of a bomb-laden F-105D prior to a combat mission over North Vietnam in 1965. (USAF)

Armourers maintaining the M61A1 Vulcan cannon of an F-105F. (USAF)

Haiphong, so it was of critical importance for the flow of supplies from Haiphong inland. It was one of five rail and road routes identified in the JCS April 1964 list as main target choices, but it was not until 11 August 1967 when it was unexpectedly released from the restricted target list. The target clearance was sent to the 355th TFW with the order to attack that day. The day's load of 750 lb bombs was hastily replaced by 3,000 lb M118 bombs and the strike was planned for the afternoon. Col. Robert White, former X-15 test pilot and astronaut (the USAF awarded astronaut wings to any pilot who had exceeded 50 miles altitude) and deputy commander of the 355th TFW, was appointed the mission leader. The commander of the 333rd TFS, Lt Col. William Norris, was the mission planner. Col. White selected the most experienced pilots and five F-105 flights of the 355th TFW took off for the mission, supported by an Iron Hand flight and bomber flights from 388th TFW, led by 469th TFS CO, Lt Col. Harry Schurr, and bomber flights from 8th TFW, led by Col. Robert Olds. The strike package arrived at the target at 15:58 and executed a perfect attack despite heavy AAA fire, breaching three spans of the bridge. The Iron Hand flight, led by Lt. Col James McInerney, took out two SAM sites and neutralised four others. Despite heavy defences, no aircraft was lost. Col. White, Col. Olds and Lt Col. McInerney were awarded Air Force Crosses for that mission. A follow-up strike was ordered for the next day. This also succeeded, putting the bridge out of use for two months, although F-105D (62-4278), flown by Capt. Thomas Norris from the 469th TFS, was shot down. The pilot ejected into captivity.

The North Vietnamese were experts in quick repairs and the bridge was again in use by October. On 25th of that month a force of 21 Takhli F-105Ds severed two spans for the loss of one aircraft. Two attacks, conducted on 14 and 18 December, put the bridge out of use until the bombing halt in November 1968.

The MiG encounters

For two years of Rolling Thunder, North Vietnamese airfields were off-limits for US aircraft. American pilots were allowed to engage North Vietnamese fighters only in the air, after positive visual identification. Therefore the NVAF, operating a small number of fighters, chiefly obsolete in comparison with US aircraft, developed very effective 'hit and run' tactics of fighter attacks, using ground-controlled interception (GCI) to direct them into ideal attack positions and evade MiGCAP flights (initially F-100D Super Sabres and F-104C Starfighters, later F-4

F-105Ds dropping bombs in level flight. (USAF)

Phantoms), escorting the strike packages. On ground they were safe, because until April 1967 attacks on North Vietnamese air bases were strictly forbidden. However, the F-105s were not entirely defenceless. During Rolling Thunder, F-105 pilots claimed 27.5 North Vietnamese MiG-17 fighters shot down (one kill was shared with an F-4D Phantom crew). The first F-105 pilot to score a MiG kill was Major Fred Tracy, the CO of 421st TFS on 29 June 1966 near Hanoi.

The MiG-17 was smaller and more agile, yet much slower than the F-105. It was armed with two 23 mm and one slow-firing 37 mm cannon, and ammunition supply allowed for 5 seconds of firing. The MiG pilots were tasked primarily with disrupting F-105 bombing attacks. When an F-105 formation was jumped by MiGs before reaching the targets, the Thunderchief pilots had to jettison the external stores and only then they could make use of the F-105's speed and run off the chasing fighters. Engaging in dogfights with more agile MiGs was not recommended, but if a MiG appeared in front of a Thunderchief, its pilot could take the chance. From December 1966 the F-105s carried AIM-9B Sidewinder heat-seeking missiles, but the primary weapon of choice in air-to-air engagements was the M61A1 Vulcan cannon and all but three kills were achieved with the gun. Guns of both aircraft had the effective range of up to about 900 m (3,000 ft). The MiG-17s, flying at their maximum speed vibrated heavily, which dispersed the cannon shells and the primitive ASP-4NM gunsight and thick, heavily-framed bulletproof windscreen limited forward visibility, which did not make aiming easier. On the other hand, the F-105 was an extremely stable gun platform and the Vulcan cannon fired 89 rounds per second in a concentrated stream. The total firing time was about 11 seconds, but the cannons had a tendency to jam, which cost many potential kills. The complex dual purpose sight was usually set in the bombing mode and re-switching it to the air-to-air mode was a quite complex and time-consuming process, often costing a kill opportunity, so the pilots often tried to get as close as possible to the MiG and fire the Vulcan cannon from minimum distance, when the enemy fighter was just in front of the F-105's nose. Usually the slower MiG-17s attacked low-flying, bomb-laden F-105 strike formations, while faster, supersonic MiG-21s, which appeared in larger numbers in the latter half of 1966, engaged the MiGCAP fighters or Wild Weasels. The Mach 2 MiG-21 was a much tougher opponent for the F-105, as the speed of both aircraft was comparable and the lighter MiG accelerated faster. When the F-105 pilot used afterburner, he became an easier target for the MiGs' heat-seeking R-3S ('AA-2 Atoll') missiles, but he could outmanoeuvre the MiG by pulling back on the throttle and deploying airbrakes, causing the attacking fighter to overshoot. Fifteen F-105s were shot down by MiG-21s, the first being 59-1725, flown by the commander of the 354th TFS, Lt Col. Don Asire, on 8 December 1966. The MiG-17s shot down seven Thunderchiefs. Since the MiGs could be engaged only when airborne, on 2 January 1967 the 8th TFW conducted Operation 'Bolo' – a plan devised by Col. Robin Olds, CO of 8th TFW, to lure the MiG-21s into an ambush. The F-4 Phantoms of 8th TFW feigned a group of bomb-laden F-105s, using their usual flight routes, altitudes, call signs and radio commands. When the MiGs took off to intercept an easy prey, they were attacked by missile-armed Phantoms, which shot down seven of them (half of the entire inventory) for no loss.

1967 was the year of heaviest MiG kills by F-105 pilots. On March 10 Capt. Max Brestel from the 354th TFS became the first USAF double MiG killer in Vietnam. On 19 April pilots from the 355th TFW shot down four MiG-17s and damaged one during the raid on Xuan Mai army barracks near Hanoi. The first one was shot down by the F-105F Wild Weasel crew of the Iron Hand flight, Maj. Leo Thorsness and Capt. Harold Johnson.

Gun camera image of the MiG-17 victory by F-105 pilot Maj. Ralph Kuster Jr. on 5 June 1967. (USAF)

Maj. Roy Dickey from the 469th TFS, 388th TFW shot down a MiG-17 on 4 December 1966. (USAF)

For their actions during that mission they were awarded the Medal of Honor and Air Force Cross respectively. Three others were shot down by pilots of strike flights. Pilots of one of the strike flights claimed two more MiGs, but these claims were not confirmed due to the lack of gun camera records.

On 13 May during heavy raids on Yen Vien railway yards, seven MiG-17 fighters were shot down, five of them by F-105 pilots – three with Vulcan cannons and two with AIM-9B Sidewinder missiles. On 23 August 1967 1st David B. Waldrop shot down two MiG-17s, although he was credited with only one confirmed and one probable victory. The last two MiG-17 kills by F-105 crews were scored on 19 December 1967 by two Wild Weasel crews from 357th TFS.

F-105 pilots

USAF pilots were required to fly 100 combat missions over North Vietnam before they could be rotated back to the US or another non-combat assignment. Missions flown over Laos, consisting of interdiction on the Ho Chi Minh trail and support of the Royal Laotian Army in combat with Pathet Lao insurgents, did not count towards the 'magic hundred', although they also were quite hazardous.

The first Thunderchief pilots to arrive in SEA were experienced and aggressive F-105 'drivers' from Japan and later US-based units, often volunteering for the combat assignments. When two F-105 wings were permanently moved to Thailand, the pilots came from the squadrons based in the US, mostly at McConnell. Losses were replaced with young lieutenants, like Ed Rasimus, fresh from F-105 conversion. When the McConnell pilots finished their tours in spring 1966, they were replaced by former F-105 instructors from Nellis and experienced pilots from combat squadrons based in Germany.

Heavy losses and the policy of sending pilots who had completed the mandatory 100-mission tour back to the US meant that, as early as mid-1966, a severe shortage of qualified F-105 pilots occurred. To solve this problem the USAF command devised the 'universally assignable pilot', which meant that every rated pilot was expected to be able to fly any type of aircraft. Bomber, transport and tanker pilots, as well as UPT instructors and staff officers, were sent on F-105 conversion courses. Since they were 'experienced', it was believed that the conversion course could be shortened to 4.5 months/60 flight hours. Unnecessary aspects of the training programme, primarily nuclear weapon delivery techniques, were skipped. The number of trainees in classes was increased twice, which gave a fourfold increase of available pilots. This idea did not, however, produce good results, as Ed Rasimus wrote:

Below, left:
Ground crews change the engine of an F-105D. Intense combat operations in the hot and humid climate of South-East Asia wore the engines out very quickly, and frequent engine changes were necessary to minimise the risks of failures. (USAF)

Below:
First Lieutenant Karl Richter from the 421st TFS, 388th TFW making a preflight check of his aircraft with the crew chief. (USAF)

"The problem was that many of these pilots couldn't deal with the speed, complexity or tactics of the mission. There is a lot of difference between hours of autopilot with a crew of four and hands-on formation coordinated tactics in a high-threat environment. The first class of fifteen graduates arrived in SEA in June-July of 1966. Of the fifteen, only one survived to complete the tour!

Certainly some tanker, C-124 and B-52/47 pilots had the skills to succeed and they did so with great distinction, courage and honour. But, unfortunately, many more were in a situation they could not cope with and they not only endangered themselves but also those who flew with them."

Another problem was that they often had higher military ranks and, despite a lack of fighter experience, quickly became element and flight leads although they were often not sufficiently capable. They were not, therefore, always able to make quick and appropriate decisions, leading to their younger, but more experienced, wingmen taking over command of the mission.

Weapons and tactics

A flight of four F-105Ds armed with M117 bombs on centreline MERs and outboard underwing pylons, refuelling en route to a target in North Vietnam. (USAF)

The F-105s carried a wide variety of ordnance. The most frequent loads were 750 lb (340 kg) M117, 1,000-lb (454 kg) Mk-83, 500-lb (227 kg) Mk-82, 250-lb (113 kg) or Mk-81 high-explosive bombs. Against hardened targets, such as bridges, 3,000-lb (1,360 kg) M118 bombs were used. Napalm, unguided rockets and AGM-12 Bullpup guided missiles were also occasionally used. When tackling SAM sites, AGM-45 Shrike anti-radiation missiles and CBU-24 cluster bombs were used, and for protection against enemy fighters AIM-9B infra-red homing air-to-air missiles were carried. As the SAM threat increased, QRC-160 jamming pods were carried on the outboard underwing pylons. Late F-105F and F-105G Wild Weasels were capable of carrying AGM-78 Standard ARM missiles.

Two F-105Ds, carrying M117 bombs and QRC-170 jamming pods, prepare for take-off from Takhli. (USAF

Two F-105Ds armed with Mk 82 bombs en route to the target. (USAF)

Two F-105Ds from the 333rd TFS (top) and 354th TFS (bottom), armed with AGM-12C Bullpup missiles, approach a tanker in 1969. (USAF)

For an F-105D on a typical bombing mission the usual load was six M117 bombs on the centreline MER and another two bombs of the same type or smaller on the outboard under-wing pylons. Instead of bombs, AIM-9B Sidewinder and jamming pods were often carried on the outboard pylons, especially during the later stages of Rolling Thunder. The two inboard pylons were occupied with 450 US gal drop tanks. While attacking hardened targets, two M118 bombs were carried on the outboard pylons and a 650 gal drop tank was carried on the centreline pylon.

The weapon loads were not always adequate for the task. The US effort in the Vietnam war was ruled by bureaucracy and statistics, not actual results and it sometimes appeared that the USAF was less concerned with fighting the enemy than competing with the rival service, the US Navy, in number of sorties flown. This often meant sending large numbers of aircraft with inappropriately small weapon loads, rather than fewer aircraft with heavier loads, which exposed more aircraft and pilots, in order to keep the sortie count high. Ed Rasimus recalled: *"Despite regular denials in the press, in the middle of 1966 we were deep in a bomb shortage. We didn't have adequate supplies of our favoured general-purpose bombs, the M117 750-pound bomb or the low-drag Mk-82 500-pounder. To compensate for the shortages and to keep our sortie counts competitive with our opponent, the US Navy (!), we carried all sorts of strange munitions. There were rockets and finned napalm, mines, and occasionally we were sent on missions into North Vietnam armed only with the Vulcan cannon. Among the strangest loads, however, was the AGM-12C, the Super Bullpup."*[1]

The USAF used two variants of the Bullpup missile: smaller AGM-12B with 250-lb (110 kg) warhead and larger AGM-12C with 970 lb (440 kg) warhead. The AGM-12B soon proved to be rather useless, so the larger AGM-12C was usually used.

"Big or small, the Bullpup was no favourite of the pilots." Ed Rasimus continues. *"To guide the missile properly, you had to set up at high altitude and establish a medium-angle dive towards the target. When the missile was fired, the pilot had to fly his airplane with his right hand and correct the missile with his left. (...) A proper delivery required exceptional coordination. During the delivery the pilot had to concentrate on the missile's flight to the target which meant that his airplane had a long, predictable flight path in areas with heavy defences. With your attention fixed on the missile you couldn't look around for SAMs or guns and the high altitude meant that you could fire the weapon only in exceptionally good weather."*[2]

F-105D-25-RE (61-0176) 'The Jolly Roger' from 357th TFS, 355th TFW, armed with AGM-12C Bullpup missiles. (USAF)

The AGM-12B was fired directly from the underwing launcher. The AGM-12C, with much more powerful rocket motor, was released like a bomb and after the release a cable attached to the launcher activated the rocket motor to avoid a destabilizing effect on the airplane. It did not always work properly. On 27 July 1966 Capt. James R. Mitchell from 421st TFS, flying F-105D (60-0045), had a serious accident when firing an AGM-12C. The front shackle, attaching the missile to the pylon, hung up which caused the missile to rotate around it. The cable fired the

1 Rasimus, Ed, *When thunder rolled: An F-105 Pilot over North Vietnam*, Presidio Press 2003, p.143.
2 Ibidem

Black smoke billowing during a cartridge engine start-up. (USAF)

An F-105D being prepared for a combat mission at Takhli. (USAF)

rocket motor and the missile hit the wing and exploded, tearing the wing to the main spar. Mitchell managed to nurse the crippled plane back to Thailand and ejected.

The usual mission employed visual dive bombing techniques. US aircraft usually operated in four-ship flights, consisting of two pairs, called elements. Two-ship formations were sent against targets of lesser significance. Tactics varied over time and often depended on individual flight leaders. Early in the war the ingress was often flown at treetop level, in mid-1966 the 388th TFW adopted ingress at medium altitude, around 4,500 ft (1,500 m) above ground level for easier navigation, better lookout and to avoid small arms fire. The cruise speed was always a multiple of 60, 480 or 540 miles per hour, for easy calculation of miles/minute, with acceleration to 600 mph just prior to the bombing run. For the bombing run the aircraft took a steep climb with afterburner to about 10,000 ft (the 'pop-up' manoeuvre) and rolled for 30 – or 45-degree dive. After bomb release they recovered at full afterburner, to get out of the target area as quickly as possible and rejoin the formation. Sometimes pilots strafed targets of opportunity, such as trucks, on the way back, but it was a risky practice.

750-lb M117 bombs on loaders prepared for loading onto an F-105D at Takhli. (USAF)

Armourers loading 750-lb M117 bombs with an MJ-1 loader onto a centreline MER on an F-105D at Takhli. (USAF)

Armourers prepare 750-lb M117 bombs for loading onto an F-105F Wild Weasel at Takhli. (USAF)

F-105Ds recovering from a dive bomb pass. (USAF)

A typical Route Package 6 mission involved four or five four-ship F-105 bomber flights, one or two four-ship Iron Hand SAM-suppression flights, two four-ship MiGCAP fighter escort flights, two or three EB-66 electronic warfare aircraft providing standoff electronic counter-measures, and eight to ten KC-135 aerial tankers.

To continue the bombing campaign when the weather deteriorated, pathfinder aircraft were used, such as RB-66B Destroyers, codenamed *Brown Cradle*, which led F-105 flights using their K-5 radar bombsights. The F-105s dropped their bombs in level flights on a signal from the RB-66. From May 1966 this was replaced by another, similar, tactic called Combat Skyspot. This was ground-directed bombing, in which the pathfinder aircraft (usually a F-100 Super Sabre) received signals from AN/MSQ-77 Bomb Directing Central, whose algorithm continuously predicted bomb impact points during the radar track while the AN/MSQ-77's control commands adjusted the aircraft's course. The pathfinder gave the signal release for the bomber aircraft. In 1966, five AN/MSQ-77 Bomb Directing Centrals were established in South Vietnam, and one in northern Thailand. Their range covered the territory of South Vietnam and parts of Laos, and the southern part of North Vietnam. In November 1967 Lima Site 85 was established in north-eastern Laos, near the North Vietnamese border. It covered most of the northern part of North Vietnam.

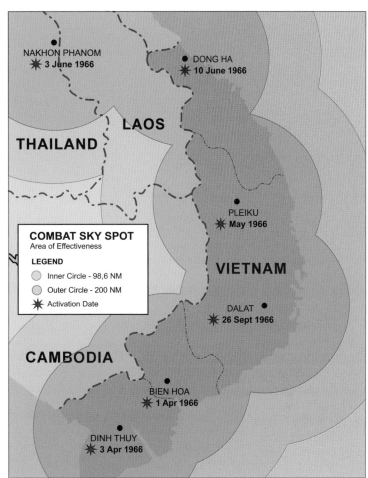

Locations of AN/MSQ-77 Bomb Directing Centrals.

Two F-105Ds led by an F-100 pathfinder on a Combat Skyspot mission. (USAF)

The SAM threat and Wild Weasels

The North Vietnamese, aided by the Soviets and Chinese, developed a very efficient air defence system, including all types of weapons from small arms, possessed by virtually every peasant, through visually and radar-directed artillery of 23 mm, 37 mm, 57 mm, 85 mm and 100 mm calibre, to S-75 *Dvina* (SA-2 Guideline) radar-guided surface-to-air missiles (SAM). On 24 July 1965 a USAF F-4C was the first victim to fall to an S-75 missile. The SAM sites had a very characteristic rose-like shape and could be spotted from the air, even when they were under construction, but the Rules of Engagement (RoE) banned attacking them until they were observed firing a missile, for fear of killing Soviet advisors operating the sites. To provide electronic protection against the radar-guided missiles, EB-66E and RB-66C electronic warfare aircraft were brought into the theatre as early as April 1965. The F-105s began flying SEAD (suppression of enemy air defence) missions, mostly using napalm and unguided rockets, but without monitoring the missile guidance radar activity these were extremely dangerous and quite ineffective. To solve this problem the USAF fielded specially modified F-100F Super Sabre aircraft, fitted with electronic equipment to detect and locate enemy radars, with a crew of two, consisting of the pilot and the Electronic Warfare Officer (EWO), who operated the detection

An early hunter-killer team: an F-105F Wild Weasel armed with AGM-45 Shrike missiles on the outboard and Mk 117 750-lb bomb on the inboard pylons and an F-105D armed with six 500-lb Mk 82 bombs on the centreline MER. (USAF)

An F-105D over Hanoi. (USAF)

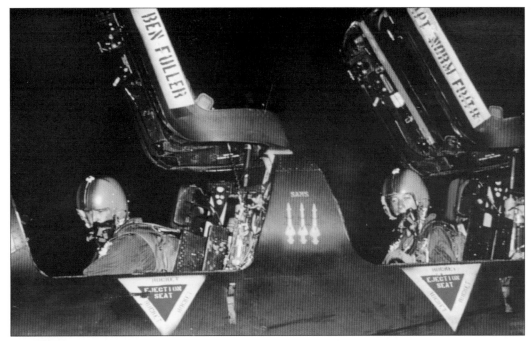

equipment. The initial four F-100F Wild Weasels were deployed to Korat in December 1965, followed by a further three in February 1966. The first successful attack on a SAM site took place on 22 December 1965 by Capt. Allen Lamb (pilot) and Capt. Jack Donovan (EWO), who marked a camouflaged SAM site for a flight of four F-105Ds from 421st TFS, which destroyed it with 2.75in rockets and Vulcan cannons. From April 1966 the Wild Weasels carried passive radar homing AGM-45 Shrike anti-radiation missiles, which could locate and destroy the SNR-75 (Fan Song) guidance radars. This greatly improved the efficiency of SEAD missions, codenamed 'Iron Hand', not only by destroying the radars, but also by forcing their crews to shut them down.

Combat attrition and incompatibility with the F-105 due to lower speed and lack of advanced avionics forced the replacement of F-100Fs by the F-105F Wild Weasel (see Chapter 4). The initial five F-105F Wild Weasels arrived at Korat on 28 May 1966. The first successful attack on a GCI radar using 2.75in unguided rockets was made on 7 June.

In July 1966 further 18 F-105Fs were converted to the Wild Weasel role and assigned to both wings based at Korat and Takhli. They usually flew as pathfinders/flight leaders for F-105D strike aircraft. Typically a 'Weasel' F-105F, armed with AGM-45 Shrike anti-radiation missiles, led a flight of three F-105Ds, one of which (number 2) was also armed with Shrike missiles and fired them following the leading Weasel towards SAM-guidance radars, while numbers 3 and 4 were armed with cluster or GP bombs. The 'Iron Hand' flights flew ahead of the strike package, trying to neutralise the enemy air defence, covered the attack and egress of the strike force. The motto of the 'Wild Weasels' was 'First in, last out'. In July 1966, when the F-100F detachment ended, the Weasels at Korat were assigned as a flight to the recently activated 13th TFS and, together with the squadron's F-105Ds, flew 'Iron Hand' missions. This squadron was disbanded due to losses in October 1967 and its activities were transferred to the 44th TFS (reformed from the 421st TFS), which flew a mix of F-105Ds and Fs in strike and Wild Weasel roles from Korat until October 1969, when it was reassigned to the 355th TFW. At Takhli the F-105F Wild Weasels were assigned as the fifth 'E' flight within each of the squadrons of the 355th TFW, beginning with the 354th TFS.

The tactics varied and were often devised in the field, on the basis of previous experience. The lineup of Iron Hand flights was also diverse, depending on the task and availability of aircraft – sometimes these were one F-105F Wild Weasel, leading three F-105Ds, sometimes two F-105Fs as element (pair) leads, with F-105Ds flying wing, sometimes the entire Iron Hand flight consisted of F-105Fs. Usually the Weasels circled on two separate orbits near the SAM site, with one element pointed towards the potential threat, attempting to draw the fire of the SAMs off the strike force. When SAMs were fired, usually in salvos of three, the Weasels evaded using the standard technique of a split-S dive, followed by a reverse split-S climb, which required perfect timing and nerves of steel. Later the tactics changed from loss-prone attacks on SAM sites as the primary task, to jamming the guidance radars to prevent launches and reduce the SAM effectiveness. The Shrike missiles provided standoff capability to some degree, but their effectiveness was also only about 15 per cent, and hits were often not visible. The best method

to determine whether the missile hit the target was to measure the time of the missile's flight to check whether the radar signal went off the air at the end of that time.

The North Vietnamese quickly learned how to defend against the Wild Weasels. They coordinated missile guidance radars with long-range GCI or early warning radars and kept them off the air, but warm. When the long-range radars warned about an incoming US strike force, the guidance radars went on air for a brief moment to verify the aiming and launch and switched off immediately.

The SAMs, like the MiGs, not only inflicted losses but also disrupted the bombing raids, because when a launch was observed, the F-105s jettisoned their ordnance and dived to low level, trying to outmanoeuvre the missile. To reduce losses and increase effectiveness of the strikes, the F-105 wings began to use QRC-160 jamming pods, carried on the outboard underwing pylon, on an increasingly large scale. Carefully planned formations, with aircraft maintaining proper vertical and horizontal separation, enabled the strike force to deny altitude, bearing and range information to enemy air defence radars. Although the pod occupied one pylon, making it useless for weapons, overall more ordnance could be delivered instead of jettisoned when the jamming pod was carried.

Wild Weasel pilots (known as 'nose gunners') were recruited from high time, experienced F-105 'drivers', while the Electronic Warfare Officers (known as 'bears') were mostly volunteers from Strategic Air Command's B-52 bomber crews. The pairings were usually fixed, since each crew developed their own system of communicating and understanding without words. The

SAM sites being destroyed. (USAF)

Wild Weasel sorties were among the most hazardous combat missions ever flown. The EWO in particular was put under enormous physical and psychological strain, having to monitor threat signals and missile launches while sitting in the rear cockpit of a violently manoeuvring jet aircraft.

The Iron Hand missions were the most dangerous of all flown during the Vietnam War, and Wild Weasel crews were often awarded the highest decorations, including the Medal of Honor and Air Force Cross.

On 10 March 1967 Captains Merlyn Dethlefsen and Kevin 'Mike' Gilroy from the 354th TFS were flying number three in a 'Lincoln' Iron Hand flight tasked with neutralising enemy defences, ahead of a strike force attacking the Thai Nguyen steel plant. On the first pass Lincoln Lead (F-105F 63-8335, piloted by Maj. David Everson and Capt. Jose Luna, who both became PoWs) was shot down by 85mm AAA fire, and Lincoln 02 was forced to withdraw with severe damage. Capt. Dethlefsen took over the command of the flight. The two Weasels were attacked by two MiG-21s. Dethlefsen fired his Shrike missiles at the SAM site and fended the attacking fighters off, making a sharp turn and flying his bomb-laden Thunderchief into a heavy barrage of AAA fire along with Lincoln 04, Major Kenneth Bell. Dethlefsen's aircraft was damaged. When they regained altitude, they were attacked by another pair of MiGs and sustained further damage, but were still flying. With the strike force and F-4 escorts egressing the target area, Dethlefsen decided to remain on scene and finish off the SAM site. He scanned the flak pattern, while his EWO pinpointed the site with his Wild Weasel electronics. Dethlefsen fired the Shrike missile to knock out the guidance radar. Along with his wingman he dived and having got visual on the site, unleashed the bombs. To make sure that the site had been destroyed they made another pass, strafing the target with cannon fire and only then headed back for Takhli. For this action, Dethlefsen was awarded the Medal of Honor and Gilroy the Air Force Cross, the next highest honour. Dethlefsen's wingman, Maj. Ken Bell, was awarded the Silver Star.

On April 19th, 1967 Major Leo Thorsness and Captain Harold Johnson from the 357th TFS in F-105F (63-8301) were leading Kingfish Iron Hand flight (three F-105F Weasel aircraft and one F-105D single-seater) on a mission against Xuan Mai army training compound, near Hanoi. Thorsness directed the second element of the Kingfish flight north, while he and his wingman manoeuvred south, forcing enemy gunners to divide their attention. Thorsness located two SAM sites and neutralised the guidance radar of one site with a Shrike missile and destroyed

Colonel Robert Scott, the commander of 355th TFW checks M117 bomb fuses before a combat mission. (USAF)

An F-105 attacking a small bridge in North Vietnam. (USAF)

Thai Nguyen steelworks, one of the most heavily defended targets in North Vietnam, under attack. (USAF)

F-105D-6-RE (59-1822) 'The Polish Glider' from 44th TFS, 355th TFW preserved at Polish Aviation Museum, Cracow. (Jarosław Dobrzyński)

F-105D-6-RE (59-1822) 'The Polish Glider' from the 44th TFS, 355th TFW, flown by Maj. Donald Kutyna, on the flightline at Takhli. (Donald Kutyna archive via MLP)

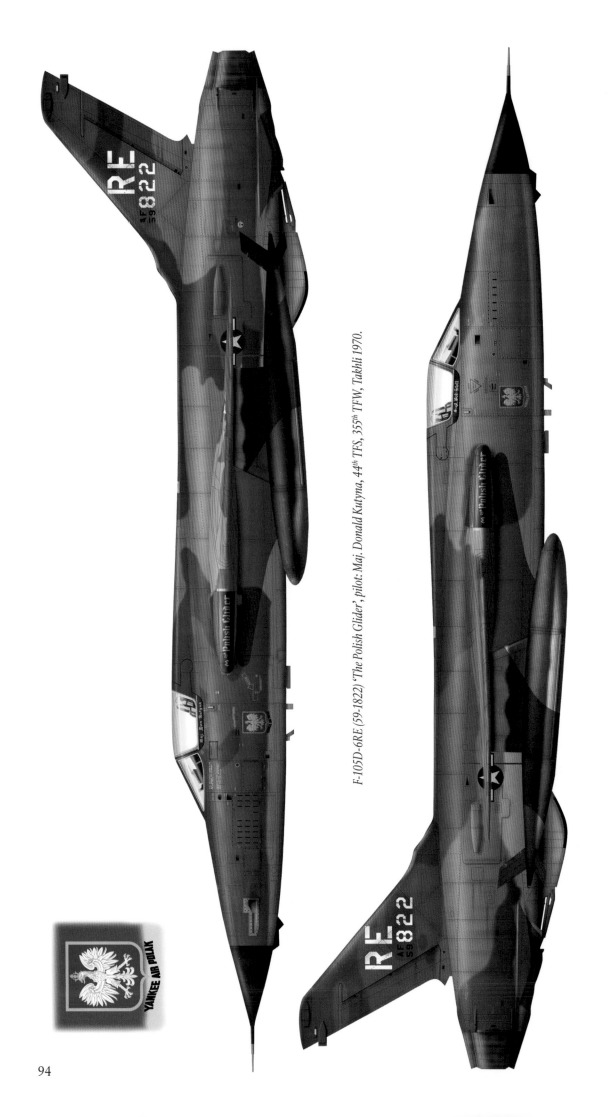

F-105D-6RE (59-1822) 'The Polish Glider', pilot: Maj. Donald Kutyna, 44th TFS, 355th TFW, Takhli 1970.

F-105D-6RE (59-1822) 'The Polish Glider', pilot: Maj. Donald Kutyna, 44th TFS, 355th TFW, Takhli 1970.

Some works of F-105 nose art were large and striking, such as the example on this F-105D-31-RE (62-4364) 'Pussy Galore', named so after a female pilot character from the James Bond movie 'Goldfinger', flown by Capt. Victor Vizcarra (right) of 354th TFS, 355th TFW, photographed while approaching the KC-135 tanker. (USAF)

the other one with cluster bombs, scoring a direct hit. Then matters took a turn for the worse. Kingfish 02 (F-105F 63-8341, crewed by Majors Thomas M. Madison and Thomas J. Sterling) was hit by flak and both crewmembers had to eject. Unknown to Thorsness, Kingfish 03 and 04 had been attacked by MiG-17s. They disengaged and headed back to base, leaving Kingfish Lead to fight alone. Thorsness circled the descending parachutes, relaying their position to a HC-130 airborne command post, codenamed Crown. His EWO spotted a MiG-17 off their right wing and Thorsness attacked it and shot it down with cannon fire. A second MiG closed

First Lieutenant David Waldrop poses with the bombs mounted on a centreline MER beneath his F-105 before a combat mission. Waldrop shot down two MiG-17 fighters. (USAF)

on their tail, but Thorsness, low on fuel, outran the attacker and headed for the rendezvous with the nearest KC-135 tanker over Laos.

Meanwhile a pair of A-1E Skyraider propeller-driven attack aircraft, codenamed 'Sandy', arrived to protect the downed airmen while they waited for the HH-3 Jolly Green Giant rescue helicopter. Thorsness, with only 500 rounds of ammunition remaining, returned to the scene to fly Rescue Combat Air Patrol (RESCAP). He spotted two MiG-17s and attacked one which flew across his path, probably shooting it down. More MiGs appeared and attacked the two Skyraiders, shooting down 'Sandy 01' (Maj. John S. Hamilton in A-1E 52-133905). Thorsness, with no ammunition left, turned back to do what he could to drive away the attacking MiGs, when 'Panda' flight of the strike force returned to the scene after having refuelled, permitting Kingfish Lead to depart the area. Panda Lead (Capt William E. Eskew) shot down a MiG, during which the surviving Sandy escaped, and he and his wingman Panda 02 (Capt. Paul A. Seymour) each damaged one of the others. Members of a third F-105 strike flight, Nitro 01 (Major Jack W. Hunt) and Nitro 03 (Maj. Ted Tolman) shot down a further two MiGs. Thorsness was heading for a rendezvous with a tanker when he heard that Panda 03 (Capt Howard L. Bodenhamer) was critically low on fuel. He calculated quickly that he had enough fuel to reach Udorn in northerm Thailand and directed the tanker towards Panda 03. When he was 60 miles of Udorn, he throttled back to idle and 'glided' toward the base, landing there with the fuel gauge showing empty. For this action he was also recommended for Medal of Honor award, and his EWO – Capt. Harold Johnson, the Air Force Cross. However, they had to wait a long time for the decorations. Eleven days later they were shot down by a MiG-21 while on their 93rd mission and spent the remainder of the war in North Vietnamese captivity. They received their medals after their return to the USA in 1973.

The Wild Weasel force was expanding and by late 1967 the number of converted F-105Fs reached 86. They were constantly upgraded with new avionics to enhance their effectiveness. The most important modification was the addition of the AGM-78A Standard ARM missile, which had a larger warhead and longer range than the AGM-45 Shrike, as well as a memory circuit enabling it to remember the location of the signal source after the radar went off air. Eight F-105Fs adapted for carrying AGM-78A missiles were delivered to the 357th TFS at Takhli between late 1967 and February 1968. On 10 March 1968 the AGM-78A missiles made their combat debut, destroying three S-75 sites near Ha Dong army barracks.

With the bombing of the North halted from November 1968, the focus of the Wild Weasels was switched to missions on the Ho Chi Minh trail in support of B-52 'Arc Light' missions and occasionally RF-4C reconnaissance missions. In October 1969 the 44th TFS, the last F-105 squadron of the 388th TFW, was reassigned to the 355th TFW at Takhli, thus all Wild Weasels were grouped at that base. The wing began receiving the ultimate Wild Weasel Thunderchief version, the F-105G, from mid-1969. Following the deactivation of the 355th TFW, they were transferred to Korat in October 1970 and initially labelled Det 1 of the 12th TFS. On 1 November 1970 the unit was reformed as 6010th Wild Weasel Squadron, on 1 December 1971 renamed 17th WWS.

Three F-105Ds undergoing final checks in the arming area before take-off for a combat mission at Takhli. (USAF)

A crew chief leaning against a 3,000 lb M118 bomb. Such ordnance was used against hardened targets, such as bridges. (USAF)

On 21 November 1970 five F-105G Wild Weasels took part in the attempt to free American PoWs (47 Weasel EWOs among them) from Son Tay prison camp. A total of 116 aircraft were involved in this operation, which went exactly to plan – except that the prisoners had been moved from the camp. During this operation one of the F-105Gs, call sign 'Firebird 3', was damaged and returned to Thailand, recovering at Udorn. 'Firebird 5', F-105G (62-4436), flown by Maj. Don Kilgus (who had scored the unconfirmed MiG-17 kill in an F-100D during the second Thanh Hoa bridge raid in April 1965) and Capt. Ted Lowry was also seriously damaged by a SAM explosion and the crew had to eject over Laos. They were picked up by a HH-53 rescue helicopter, which had been intended to evacuate the PoWs.

In late 1971 and early 17th WWS was involved in Operation *Proud Deep Alpha* against the growing network of SAM sites near the Laotian border, intended to protect traffic on the Ho Chi Minh Trail as the North Vietnamese were preparing their major incursion into South Vietnam.

In April 1972 full-scale hostilities recommenced. The USA launched Operation Linebacker I, a bombing campaign intended to force the North Vietnamese to agree a peace treaty. Missions

F-105D-10-RE (60-0504) 'Memphis Belle II' from the 357th TFS, 355th TFW, named after the 8th Air Force's most famous B-17 bomber, en route to the target after having refuelled from a KC-135 tanker. (USAF)

F-105D-10-RE (60-0504) 'Memphis Belle II' taxiing out of the revetment at Takhli, armed with two 3,000 lb M118 bombs on inboard wing pylons. (USAF)

An F-105D armed with M117 and Mk 81 bombs with fuse extenders in flight over Laos. (USAF)

against heavily defended targets around Hanoi and Haiphong became routine again. Now the Wild Weasels often supported B-52 raids against targets in North Vietnam. During the four-year recess in bombing, North Vietnamese defences had been massively reinforced. The 17th WWS was the only Wild Weasel unit in the theatre and on 7 April it received support in the form of the Det 1 561st TFS/23 TFW, freshly arrived from McConnell with a strength of 12 F-105Gs. The F-105Gs operated now in hunter-killer teams with F-4E Phantoms, locating the SAM sites and destroying radars with Shrike and Standard missiles, while the Phantoms knocked out fragile control vans, launchers and missiles with cluster bombs. During Operation Linebacker I, which ended on 22 October 1972, four F-105G Wild Weasels were lost to enemy air defences. The last one was lost on 16 October.

When bombing resumed on 18 December 1972 under Operation Linebacker II, the Wild Weasels flew up to three missions a day, supporting strikes of B-52s at night and tactical aircraft around the clock. This support was effective, because the during the massive 11-day bombing campaign, only 15 US aircraft were lost.

After the signing of the agonisingly achieved peace treaty, the strike supports into Laos continued until 21 February 1973. The 561st TFS returned to the USA in September of that year. The last aircraft of the 17th WWS departed Thailand on 29 October 1974.

Ryan's Raiders

The F-105s operated in daylight, and bad weather limited their effectiveness despite advanced navigation equipment. The USAF did not at that time have an all-weather strike aircraft like the Navy's Grumman A-6A Intruder. The two-seat, swing-wing all-weather F-111A was not yet operational. Therefore in early 1967, General John D. Ryan, CiNC PACAF decided to form a special unit equipped with specially modified aircraft with two-man crews, to conduct night precision strikes under Operation Northscope. This unit, named Ryan's Raiders, was officially formed on 4 March 1967 at Yokota AB, Japan, equipped with modified F-105F Wild Weasels (this modification was known as Commando Nail – see Chapter 4). The initial batch of ten front-seaters (pilots) for Operation Northscope were pilot instructors and the back-seaters were pilots drawn from replacements intended for combat wings operating from Thailand, so the initial Raider crews consisted of two pilots, not a pilot and B/N or EWO.

A training programme was devised, consisting of a quick but intense course on the operation of the R-14A radar and radar bombing techniques, then a 10-hour refresher course on the radar, toss bomb computer and radar image interpretation for both crew members, followed by 12 training flights in Japan. The Raider missions were originally devised to be flown at altitudes between 10,000 and 15,000 feet, but Gen. Ryan instead called for 'low profile missions' between 500-2,000 ft.

The first Raider aircraft and crews arrived at Korat on 24 April 1967 and were assigned to the 13th TFS. They flew their first mission on 26 April, a night strike against the Ron ferry on the Red River and Yen Bai railroad yards. Further two contingents of four crews each arrived on 8 and 22 May. Over the next 80 days they flew 98 missions into RP 5 and 6A.

Since the Raider aircraft were Wild Weasel F-105Fs, the PACAF changed the makeup of the crews from two pilots to a pilot and an EWO, the latter of whom could function as the B/N and operate the SEAD equipment for defensive purposes. That posed a problem, because most Weasel EWOs were ex-SAC EWOs, not qualified as bombardiers or navigators. These crews had to complete a thorough radar bombing training

Left: One of the 'Ryan's Raiders' crews. (USAF)

F-105D-31-RE (62-4405) armed with two M118 bombs awaiting its turn for a hook-up with the KC-135 en route to the target. (USAF)

An F-105 trails smoke just after a near-interception by an S-75 (SA-2) missile. The missile missed the aircraft, but the proximity fuse detonation threw fragments over a wide area. The photo was taken by the rear-facing combat camera of another F-105, jinking to avoid enemy fire. Note bombs on the centreline MER, visible on the left side of the photo. (USAF)

course to be qualified for the Raider missions. The first pilot/EWO crews arrived at Korat on 17 July 1967.

The weapons load was usually standard for the F-105s in SEA – six M117 bombs on the centreline MER, with some fitted with fuse extenders and at least one having a 24-hour delayed action fuse. The aircraft also carried a pair of ECM pods and two 450-gallon underwing tanks. One ECM pod was usually replaced by an AIM-9B Sidewinder infra-red homing missile on the starboard outer wing pylon for protection against NVAF fighters, and although no MIGs were encountered by Raider crews, two pilots were credited with destroying anti-aircraft searchlights with the heat-seeking missiles.

With the bomb load, two external fuel tanks, ECM pod and Sidewinder missile, the Raider F-105Fs were highly overloaded on take-off, even before the internal fuel tanks were full. In daylight operations this was no problem, since the aircraft could take-off with low fuel and top off the tanks on a rendezvous with a tanker once airborne. Refuelling at night or in bad weather was extremely dangerous, so most Raider missions took off at above maximum gross weight. They still had to refuel over northern Laos, but only once.

Understandably, the Raider missions were very dangerous. During the first month of operations two aircraft were lost. One probably hit the ground during a low-level penetration into North Vietnam due to malfunction of the terrain-following radar, and the other was shot down by AAA over Kep.

A typical Raider mission was flown at about 10,000 ft before crossing the North Vietnamese border, after the rendezvous with the tanker. Crossing the border, the Raider pilot descended to an altitude of about 500 ft below the ridge line, changing heading every five minutes en route to the target, flying at about 450 kt.

After having reached the Initial Point, the Raider pilot commenced the bombing run, accelerating to 500 kt and climbing to 1,000 ft for bomb release, and after releasing the bomb, egressed the target area, while the backseater reverted from B/N to EWO role, monitoring the ER-142 for enemy tracking radar activity. During this phase an EB-66 from Takhli would orbit just outside North Vietnam to provide long-range warnings of SAM, AAA and MiG threats to the Raider. A regular Wild Weasel aircraft also took part in the mission, providing defence suppression on the way home.

On 4 October 1967 another aircraft was lost during a night attack on Phu Tho rail yard and the low-level Raider missions were halted. Between 26 April and 4 October 1967 Raider crews flew a total of 415 missions, mostly to Route Package 5 and 6A. From August 1967 many Raider aircraft were diverted to Wild Weasel support of B-52 missions.

After the 4 October loss, Raider missions were limited to interdiction raids into Route Package 1 in the southern part of North Vietnam, which also were hazardous, but did not require in-flight refuelling due to the closer proximity to Korat. The Raiders were also tasked with daylight pathfinder missions, known as *Commando Nail Papa*, when weather conditions prevented a standard visual bombing run. A pair of Raider F-105Fs would lead the strike package

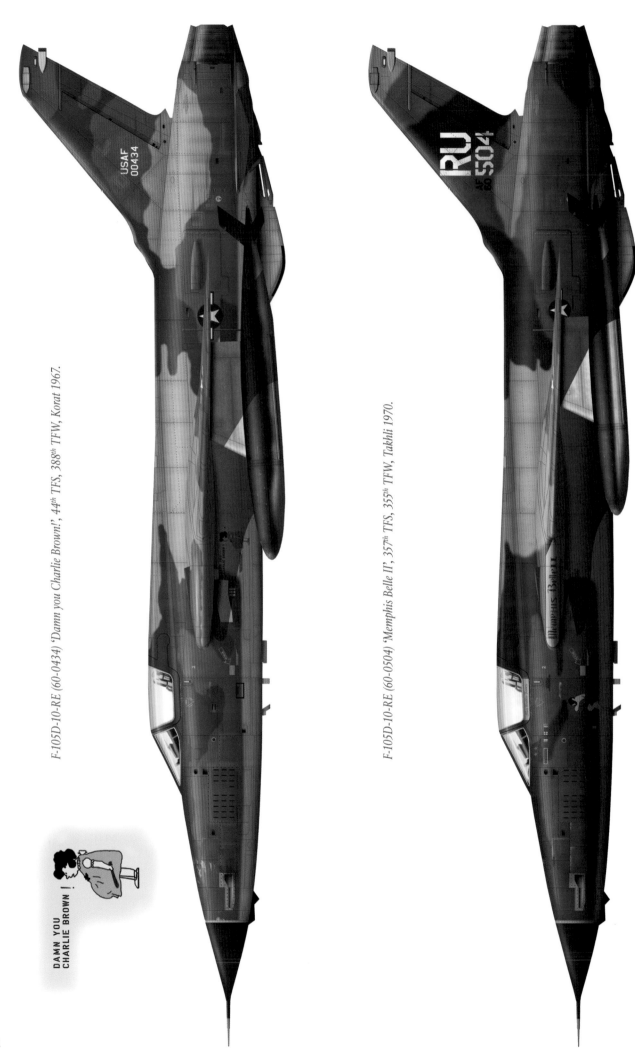

F-105D-10-RE (60-0434) 'Damn you Charlie Brown!', 44th TFS, 388th TFW, Korat 1967.

F-105D-10-RE (60-0504) 'Memphis Belle II', 357th TFS, 355th TFW, Takhli 1970.

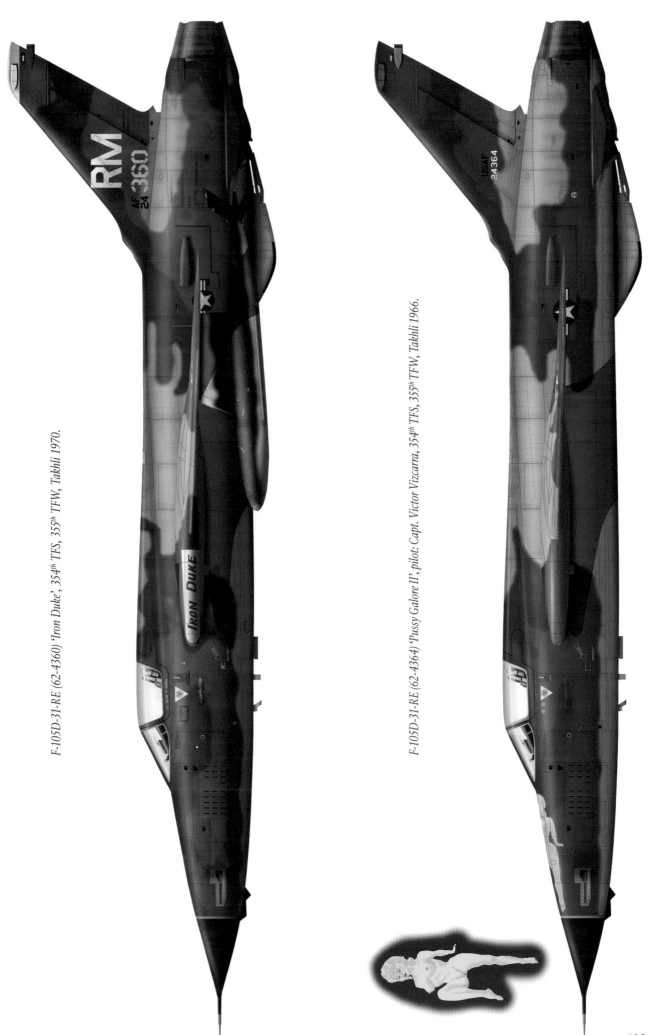

F-105D-31-RE (62-4360) 'Iron Duke', 354th TFS, 355th TFW, Takhli 1970.

F-105D-31-RE (62-4364) 'Pussy Galore II', pilot: Capt. Victor Vizcarra, 354th TFS, 355th TFW, Takhli 1966.

103

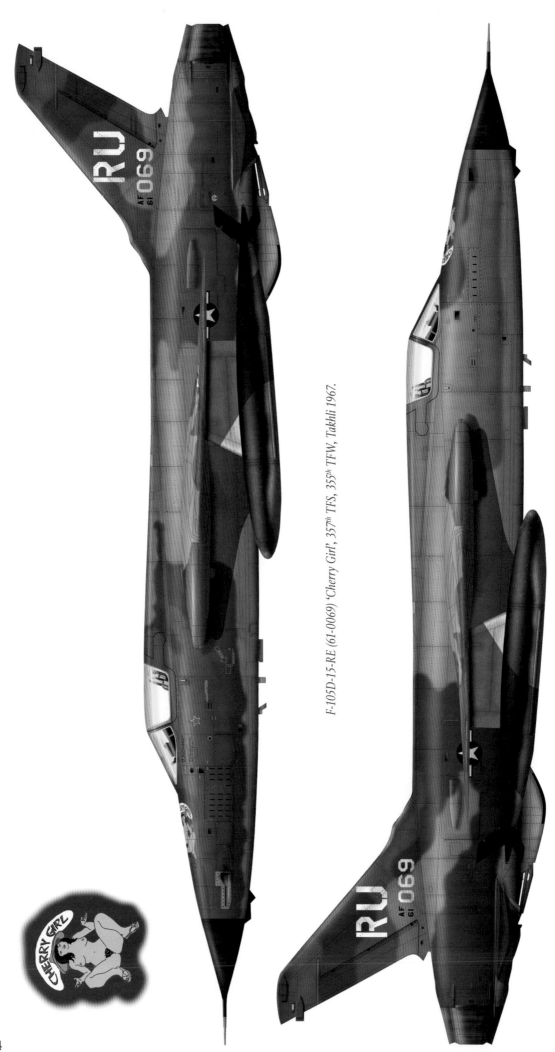

F-105D-15-RE (61-0069) 'Cherry Girl', 357th TFS, 355th TFW, Takhli 1967.

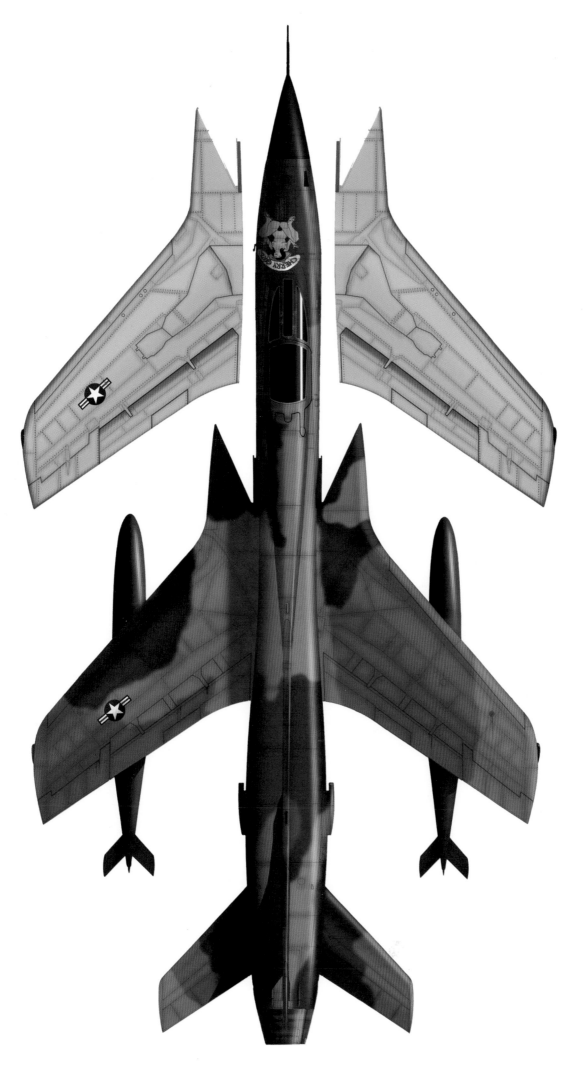

F-105D-15-RE (61-0069) 'Cherry Girl', 357th TFS, 355th TFW, Takhli 1967.

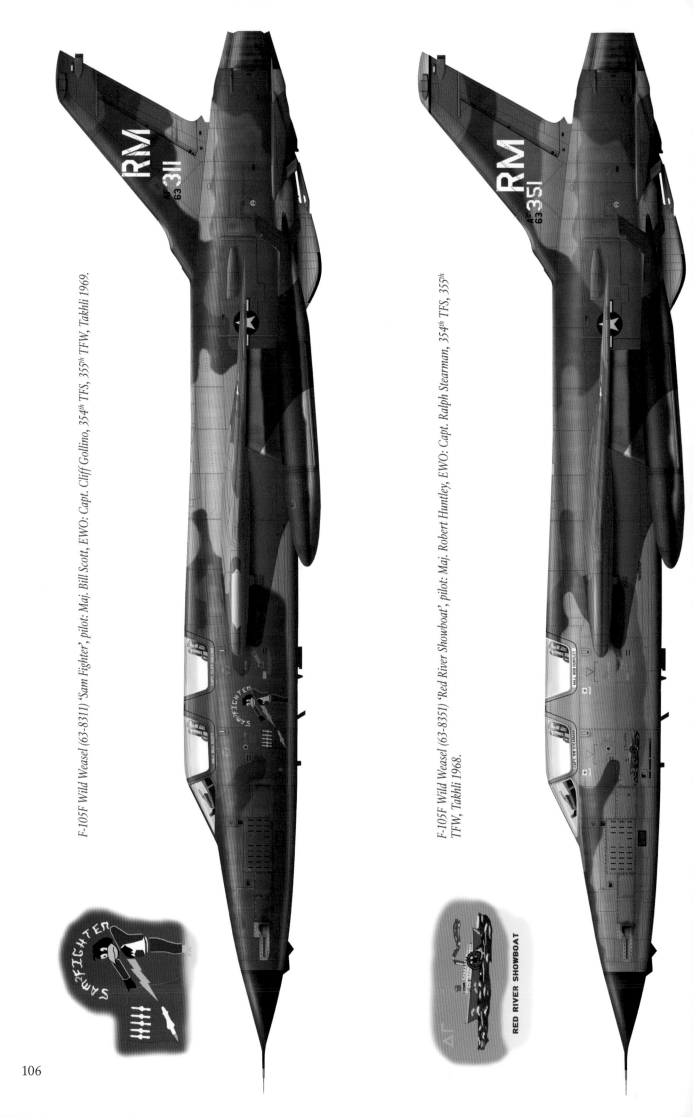

F-105F Wild Weasel (63-8311) 'Sam Fighter', pilot: Maj. Bill Scott, EWO: Capt. Cliff Gollino, 354th TFS, 355th TFW, Takhli 1969.

F-105F Wild Weasel (63-8351) 'Red River Showboat', pilot: Maj. Robert Huntley, EWO: Capt. Ralph Stearman, 354th TFS, 355th TFW, Takhli 1968.

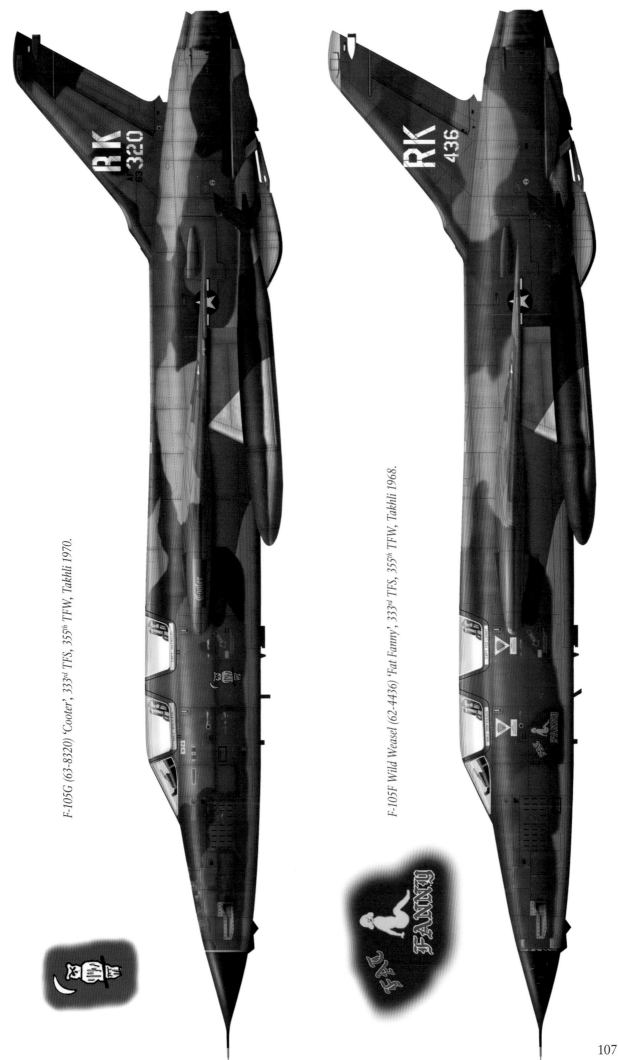

F-105G (63-8820) 'Cooter', 333rd TFS, 355th TFW, Takhli 1970.

F-105F Wild Weasel (62-4436) 'Fat Fanny', 333rd TFS, 355th TFW, Takhli 1968.

First Lieutenant Karl W. Richter from the 421st TFS, 388th TFW completed his first 100-mission tour in October 1966 and volunteered for another one. He was shot down by AAA over RP1 on his 198th mission on 28 July 1967. He ejected, but suffered severe injuries on landing in rocky terrain and died aboard the rescue helicopter. (USAF)

Other examples of battle damage sustained by the F-105s over North Vietnam. (USAF)

of 16 F-105Ds. Although successful, these missions were vulnerable to SAM attacks, since the formation had to spread out to obtain an acceptable bombing pattern, which also loosened the ECM protection. Flying above the overcast gave the pilots no warning of a SAM launch until the last moment, when the missile emerged from the cloud deck, which was usually too late for evasive action.

In 1968 the Raider missions ceased and the remaining aircraft were transferred to Wild Weasel squadrons for regular SEAD missions. Despite its limited effectiveness, the Ryan's Raiders' programme was deemed a success, paving the way for future F-111A precise night strikes of single aircraft on key targets, and night interdiction missions flown by the F-4D-equipped 497th TFS 'Night Owls'.

Mismanagement of the war

The combat effort of Operation *Rolling Thunder* was considerable, conducted at heavy cost in aircraft, aircrews, weapons and fuel supplies. Missions were flown with mixed results, sometimes good, sometimes poor, but the effects seemed to be imperceptible. Supplies continued to flow inland from North Vietnamese ports, and then to South Vietnam via Laos. Viet Cong and NVA were still operating in South Vietnam, and North Vietnamese defences were increasingly heavy and effective. The poor effectiveness of *Rolling Thunder* resulted primarily from the erroneous policy of President Johnson's administration, consisting of gradual escalation of the bombing campaign in order to force the North Vietnamese to enter peace negotiations and withdraw from South Vietnam. For this reason, and a fear of the direct involvement of China and the USSR, very strict Rules of Engagement (ROE) were imposed upon US air forces. The ROE consisted mainly of banning attacks on numerous, usually important, targets in North Vietnam, the destruction of which would have improved the chances of US victory. Leaving such

Maj. William McClelland posing, after a fortunate landing, in the hole punched out of the wing of F-105D-10-RE (60-0454) by an 85 mm AAA shell. Sometimes the F-105s could take severe punishment over hostile territory and return to base. (USAF)

Bac Giang thermal power plant bombed by F-105s. (USAF)

Three F-105Ds from the 34th TFS/388th TFW 'going downtown' in 1968. Each aircraft carries six M117 750-lb bombs on the centreline MER and an AN/ALQ-72 jamming pod on outboard underwing pylons. (USAF)

targets alone, meanwhile, exposed US aircraft to heavy losses. These rules were indexed in a thick, constantly updated book, with which every pilot had to become acquainted before flying their first combat mission. Breaching these rules could result in court martial. The targets were selected in Washington, often over a White House lunch, when the President and Secretary of Defence, sometimes aided by the Chairman of the Joint Chiefs of Staff, mulled over the military's proposed target list, picked some out, and had them relayed back down the line to Saigon and, eventually, to Korat and Takhli. Once an item became a target, it remained one. If it wasn't destroyed on the first raid, it would be attacked again and again until it was.

Air-to-air combat was also not welcome, especially early in the war, since it was considered politically inflammatory. When Capt. Don Kilgus shot down a MiG-17 (which previously had shot down an F-105D during the disastrous second Thanh Hoa Bridge raid) President Johnson stated that "he did not want any more MiGs shot down". That was one possible reason why Kilgus' claim was never confirmed. It caused great bitterness among US aircrews, who had the impression that their own government cared more about the comfort of the enemy than a quick victory with minimal losses.

As Ed Rasimus wrote in his memoirs: "*Combat restrictions were extensive, unbelievable and decidedly illogical. There was a buffer zone of twenty miles along the entire northern border of NVN and China. It was designed to avoid international incidents with China, but restricted not only the delivery of ordnance but even manoeuvring within the airspace. Although drawing a squiggly line on a map matching the convolutions of the boundary between the countries was easy, the obvious fact was that the airborne fighter pilot had few landmarks that would readily define the buffer. The result would be a considerably larger safety zone for China forcing our aircraft into a smaller, more hazardous area with much more concentrated defences.*

First Lieutenant Ed Rasimus from the 421st TFS, 388th TFW, frequently cited in this book, upon completion of his 100th mission in November 1966 at Korat. (USAF)

"*The major cities of Hanoi and Haiphong were restricted. (…) Hanoi got a ten-mile radius circle, while the port city got only five.*

"*The details of the rules for North Vietnam were the truly sticky part. (…) Carefully plotted were the sites for surface-to-air batteries. (…) They were off-limits while under construction, but could be attacked once they were completely built. To confirm that they were actually no longer under construction the SAM site had to be observed firing a missile at you. Sure, that makes a lot of sense.*

"*Enemy airfields, which were plainly marked on the maps and much easier to see than SAM sites, were also protected. No longer did we have the onerous restrictions that had frustrated Korean War fighter pilots. No Yalu River and China sanctuary. No, now we let the airfields within the battle area remain inviolate. Enemy aircraft could be engaged, but only after positive visual identification and only if they were definitely airborne. For us, there would be no dastardly attacks of aircraft in the traffic pattern or while parked on the ramp.*

F-105D (62-4338) 'Alice's Joy', the personal aircraft of Col. Jack Broughton, deputy commander of the 355ᵗʰ TFW, named after his wife, being prepared for a mission. The armourers are removing expended ammunition cartridges. (USAF)

(...) *Targets within Route Pack VI were strictly controlled by the National Command Authority, which is fighter pilot terminology for the President and the Joint Chiefs of Staff. The only targets we could strike in RP VI were ones that Washington had specifically approved. No targets of opportunity were allowed. Not even emergency jettison was approved. Adding insult to the blatantly obvious potential for injury was the restriction that the Air Force aircraft could not drop in the VI-B area without the Navy's prior approval".*[3]

Lt. Col. John Piowaty, who as a captain flew F-105 from Takhli in 1967 wrote in 'Reflections of a Thud driver' for the January-February 1983 edition of the Air University Review: *"In looking back on my experiences as an F-105 pilot in the mid-sixties, I realise that some of my strongest recollections involve the general frustration that we Thud drivers felt concerning the restrictions under which our war against the North was fought. Our rules of engagement (ROE) were defined with a rigid precision that made little sense to us at the time-and which make little more sense to me today."* He further commented: *"I remember a protected building in Route Pack I, a church we were told. My wingman, one day, bragged that he got a large warehouse. 'Not a big white building with a pitched roof?' 'Yeah. Why?' 'That was a church. We weren't supposed to hit it.' 'Well, whatever it was, I got a helluva secondary (explosion) out of it!'"*

Capt. Anthony Andrews of 34ᵗʰ TFS, 388ᵗʰ TFW, shot down on 17 October 1967 during his 27ᵗʰ mission over North Vietnam recalled: *"As General Westmoreland stated 'Although our efforts to interdict the flow of supplies is not completely successful, we nevertheless are causing the North Vietnamese to employ about 50,000 trained regular forces to maintain their air defence system'. I saw this as an admission that I was also being used as a TARGET for NVN gunners to shoot at. Worst of all, though, was the Micro-managing of our target list from the White House and poor support from higher headquarters. We were as much threatened by our own stupid politicos and their lackey officers, as we were from the enemy".*

An F-105F and F-105D taxiing upon landing following the 100ᵗʰ combat mission. Extended refuelling probes symbolise 'giving the finger to the world'. (USAF)

3 Ed Rasimus "When thunder rolled: An F-105 Pilot over North Vietnam" Presidio Press 2003, p. 64-65

Left: Lt Col. Robert Krone, the CO of the 469ᵗʰ TFS, 388ᵗʰ TFW, hands in the customary case of beer to his crew chief upon completion of his 100ᵗʰ mission at Korat on 3 June 1966. He was the first squadron commander to complete the 100-mission tour. (USAF Museum)

Captains Lamont 'Monty' Pharmer (left) and Gary Durkee of 34ᵗʰ TFS celebrate completion of their 100ᵗʰ missions over North Vietnam in August 1968. Both sit on a special 'Snoopy's doghouse' trailer, used for 100-mission parades at Korat air base (below). A scarf with the names of all 34ᵗʰ TFS pilots who completed the 100-mission tours hangs around Pharmer's neck. The hollow pineapple is filled with rum. (USAF)

The 100-mission shoulder patch. (USAF)

The most infamous case of persecuting the aircrews for alleged violation of the ROE, perfectly correlating with Andrews' opinion, was so-called *Turkestan* incident. On 2 June 1967 two pilots from the 354ᵗʰ TFS, Maj. Ted Tolman and Maj. Alonzo Ferguson, having previously attacked their assigned target, strafed enemy AAA gun positions around Cam Pha harbor, which had fired at them while they were inbound to target. The harbour was off-limits under the ROE. On the strafing run Tolman suddenly saw a large ship in the harbour roadstead. They aborted the strafing run, climbed for altitude and headed south. The ship would be in the middle of the gun camera images but the field of focus was too narrow for the film to show the ground fire coming up from all sides and that the targets of the strafing run were the gun emplacements. Tolman and Ferguson landed to refuel at Ubon because of weather and they were taken to a mandatory intelligence debriefing. Distressed by the situation, Tolman denied firing his cannon, which was a false official statement on the record, impossible to be called back. Ferguson was equally at fault by not correcting the statement. After landing at Takhli they told Colonel Jack M. Broughton, the deputy commander of the 355ᵗʰ TFW about the incident. On that day the wing commander was absent and Broughton was the acting commander. Having learned that the film from the gun camera was the only evidence against the two pilots, Broughton exposed the undeveloped film to light to destroy any evidence of a possible violation of the ROE. General John D. Ryan, PACAF commander, learned about possible attack on a ship and started investigation. On the next day the Soviets claimed that their merchant ship *Turkestan* had been

First Lieutenant David Waldrop from the 34th TFS/388th TFW celebrates his 100th mission at Korat on 4 December 1967. (USAF)

An F-105 going down in flames after being hit by enemy fire. (USAF)

bombed in Cam Pha roadstead and showed an unexploded round from the M61 cannon, allegedly from the damage on the ship. The shell could not have come from Tolman's or Ferguson's aircraft and had probably been recovered from a wreckage of another F-105 found somewhere in North Vietnam. The Pentagon denied US attack on the ship and the affair quietened down, but General Ryan, for unknown reasons continued to pursue the investigation and sought to identify the pilots involved in the incident. On 17 June he confronted Broughton at Takhli. Broughton told him that the two pilots he was looking for were Tolman and Ferguson and that he, Broughton, had destroyed the film.

The PACAF decided to put Broughton and the two majors before a court-martial to make their case a deterrent against any future violations of ROE. They were accused of conspiracy to conceal a material fact, by exposing the undeveloped film, and destruction of government property. This was in contrast with the US Navy's attitude. On 29 June two US Navy aircraft attacked another Soviet ship, *Mikhail Frunze*, in Haiphong harbour. The Department of Defence stated that the damage to the ship was inadvertent and US Navy ignored the situation, unwilling to persecute the pilots for violating the ROE.

The court-martial was held at Clark Air Base, Philippines, the headquarters of the 13th Air Force. It was presided by Col. Charles 'Chuck' Yeager, one of most famous and respected US fighter and test pilots.

With the gun camera film destroyed, there was no evidence against Tolman and Ferguson and they were acquitted of all charges, which was what Broughton intended to achieve. The court threw out conspiracy charges against Broughton, but convicted him of the lesser charges of destroying government property, imposing a fine and admonishment. Following the court martial Broughton was assigned to the Weapon System Evaluation Group in Washington, D.C., which was rather a meaningless job, a form of additional punishment for Broughton, ordered by USAF higher echelons, displeased with the court's verdict.

On 15 October an article in *Miami Herald* cited an unnamed witness, who had visited the *Turkestan* and seen holes in the upper and lower bridge, varying in diameter from 15 to 40 mm. The entry of the bullets had been

Left: The fate of so many F-105 pilots. Capt. Anthony Andrews from 34th TFS posing in front of his F-105 before a mission in 1967... (Anthony Andrews archive)

... and feeding turkeys in a PoW camp in 1968. He was shot down by AAA on his 27th mission, over Dap Cau rail yard in RP6A, on 17 October 1967 and spent 5 ½ years in North Vietnamese captivity. (Anthony Andrews archive)

horizontal rather than at a downward angle, which indicated that the ship had been shot by North Vietnamese guns firing at low-flying aircraft.

In July 1968 the Air Force Board for Correction of Military Records found the felony conviction disproportionate and administered a milder, non-judicial punishment. Following this, Broughton retired from the USAF on 31 August 1968. "*I was shot down by our own people*", he commented.

After *Rolling Thunder*

By the spring of 1967 the Secretary of Defence, Robert McNamara, and other civilian advisors, had become convinced that both Operation *Rolling Thunder* and the ground war in South Vietnam were not working and opposed the Joint Chiefs' recommendations for an increased tempo of bombing and the loosening of target restrictions. The generals claimed that *Rolling Thunder* was working, yet they still demanded fewer restrictions and heavier punch in order to make the campaign succeed. The limited objectives of US foreign policy, restricted to preventing North Vietnam from 'exporting revolution' to South Vietnam and attempting to unite the country under Communist rule, were contradictory to the military objective of total victory. The problem was 'how to defeat North Vietnam without defeating North Vietnam'.

F-105D-10-RE (60-0504) 'Memphis Belle II' from the 357th TFS, 355th TFW armed with six 500-lb Mk 82 and two 250 lb Mk 81 bombs taxiing at Takhli in 1970. (Donald Kutyna archive via MLP)

F-105D-6-RE (59-1760) 'The Underdog', from the 44th TFS, 355th TFW, armed with six 500-lb Mk 82 and two 250 lb Mk 81 bombs with fuse extenders, taxis before a mission at Takhli in 1970. (Donald Kutyna archive via MLP)

FF-105F (63-8327) 'Sweet Caroline', from the 44th TFS, 355th TFW armed with six 500-lb Mk 82 and two 250 lb Mk 81 bombs with fuse extenders, taxis before a mission at Takhli in 1970. (Donald Kutyna archive via MLP)

An F-105D with full bomb load ready for a mission at Takhli in 1966. (USAF)

F-105D-10-RE (60-0464) from the 44th TFS, 355th TFW in flight with six M117 bombs on centreline MER and two Mk 81 bombs on outboard underwing pylons. (USAF)

F-105D (62-4338) 'Alice's Joy', the personal aircraft of Col. Jack Broughton, deputy commander of the 355th TFW, named after his wife, being prepared for a mission. The armourers are removing expended ammunition cartridges. (USAF)

Colonel Jack Broughton, deputy commander of the 355th TFW, talks to his crew chief after a mission. (USAF)

The F-105F Wild Weasel (63-8301) flown by Thorsness and Johnson on the mission on April 19, 1967. (USAF)

An F-105D starting up the engine with the cartridge starter. This method was used in the SEA when launching numerous aircraft for combat missions, as it was quicker. (USAF)

Above: The most famous Wild Weasel crew, Maj. Leo Thorsness (pilot) and Capt. Harold Johnson (EWO) from the 357th TFS, 355th TFW. (USAF)

F-105G (63-8320) 'Cooter', armed with AGM-45 Shrike and AGM-78 Standard anti-radiation missiles, takes fuel from a KC-135. (USAF)

Below, left and right: Major Bob Huntley (pilot) and Captain Ralph Stearman (EWO) from the 354th TFS, 355th TFW celebrate their final mission in F-105F (63-8351) 'Red River Showboat' at Takhli in 1968. They flew 100 Iron Hand missions during 1967–68 and shot down a MiG-17. (USAF)

Political frictions lasted for a year. In February 1968 Robert McNamara was replaced by Clark Clifford, who had opposed his suggestions, but his point of view was adopted by the Secretary of State Dean Rusk. Rusk proposed limiting the bombing campaign to the 'panhandle' of North Vietnam and await Hanoi's reaction. To encourage Hanoi to enter peace negotiations, on 31 March 1968 President Johnson announced that bombing north of the 19th parallel would cease. All Air Force, Navy and Marine bombing efforts were concentrated in the area between the 17th and 19th parallels, roughly equivalent to Route Package 1. The main task was interdiction – road intersection and bridge busting, truck hunting etc. In response the

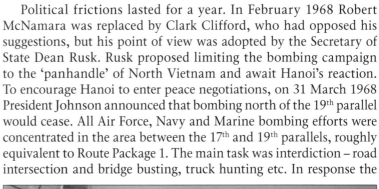

The F-105F Wild Weasel flown by Major Merlyn Dethlefsen and Capt. Mike Gilroy. (USAF)

Major Merlyn Dethlefsen and Capt. Mike Gilroy after the completion of their 100th mission over North Vietnam. (USAF)

A Wild Weasel crew, Maj. John Revak (pilot) and Maj. Stanley Goldstein (EWO) from the 44th TFS, 388th TFW, both New Yorkers, with the flag of New York City which they had received from the mayor of New York and took on a mission over North Vietnam. Note the name of the aircraft. (USAF)

Majors Revak and Goldstein in a typical Wild Weasel crew pose in front of their F-105F before a mission. The aircraft is armed with CBU-24 cluster bombs on the centreline MER. (USAF)

Two F-105Gs armed with AGM-45 Shrike missiles. (USAF)

North Vietnamese redeployed many of their AAA batteries to that area, but most SAM batteries remained in their previous locations farther north.

Hanoi, which had continuously stipulated that it would not commence negotiations unless the bombing ceased, finally agreed to meet with the Americans for preliminary talks in Paris. President Johnson ordered a complete halt to bombing of North Vietnam from 1 November 1968. Although the bombing halt was intended to be related with the progress in peace talks, eventually it lasted until the spring of 1972.

The halt of bombing of North Vietnam marked the beginning of the end of single-seat F-105 operations in SEA. A week later the 388th TFW at Korat began replacing its F-105Ds with F-4E Phantoms. The last F-105D unit of the 388th TFW was the 44th TFS, which was reassigned to the 355th TFW at Takhli in October 1969, equipped with the mix of F-105Ds and Fs. Takhli-based squadrons flew interdiction missions over Laos and South Vietnam until October 1970, when the 355th TFW was deactivated and the last 48 aircraft returned to the US. Only the two-seat Wild Weasels, for which there was no replacement, remained in the theatre.

Of the 753 F-105Ds and Fs produced, 395 were lost during the Vietnam War – 344 F-105Ds, 36 F-105Fs and 15 F-105Gs (F-105F conversions). Of them 269 were shot down by anti-aircraft guns, 35 by SAMs and 17 by enemy fighters. A further 74 were lost due to accidents and failures.

A hunter-killer team comprising F-105G Wild Weasels and F-4E Phantoms from the 388th TFW refuelling en route to the target during Operation 'Linebacker I' in 1972. (USAF)

F-105G (62-4425) (crew: Captains Jim Boyd and Kim Pepperell) landing at Korat with unexpended ordnance on the last day of Operation 'Linebacker II', 29 December 1972. (USAF)

The same F-105G (62-4425) being prepared for a mission on Korat flightline during Operation 'Linebacker' in 1972. (USAF)

F-105D-6-RE (59-1822) 'The Polish Glider' from 44th TFS, 355th TFW, flown by Maj. Donald Kutyna. The aircraft is armed with M117 and Mk 81 bombs with fuse extenders. (Donald Kutyna via MLP)

Chapter 7
Technical description

Fuselage

The fuselage was of semi-monocoque construction, consisting of four sections. The nose section contained the pressurised cockpit, avionics, the M61 gun with its ammunition supply, and the nose-wheel bay. The centre section enclosed the fuel tanks and the internal weapons bay (which was nearly 16 ft/4.88 m in length and 32 in/80 cm in depth and width) with two inward-opening doors that were cleared for operation up to Mach 2. The wing was attached at this point and two large frames took its aerodynamic load. The next section, aft of the wings, housed the J-75 engine, fuel and water tanks. The rearmost section with the empennage was detachable to enable engine changes. The empennage comprised a vertical stabiliser with rudder and all-moving horizontal stabilisers (stabilators), made of aluminium and magnesium with a steel beam backbone. At the end of this section were the distinctive four-petal airbrakes, used in various configurations for dive bombing (all four petals opened) and landing (only the lateral petals opened due to ground clearance and brake chute). The petals also opened by 9 degrees when the afterburner was engaged to allow for the larger flow of exhaust gases. An air scoop for engine compartment cooling was located at the base of the vertical stabiliser, and later two additional air scoops were added on the fuselage sides. To obtain a lighter structure, Republic used machine-milled skins of varying thickness for optimum distribution of strength and weight. This production method was costly, yet profitable, since it allowed for significant savings in the weight of the aircraft. A ventral fin to increase longitudinal stability was mounted beneath the rear fuselage, with an arresting hook, stressed to 49,000 lb (22,246 kg), that was

F-105D/F general arrangement. (USAF)

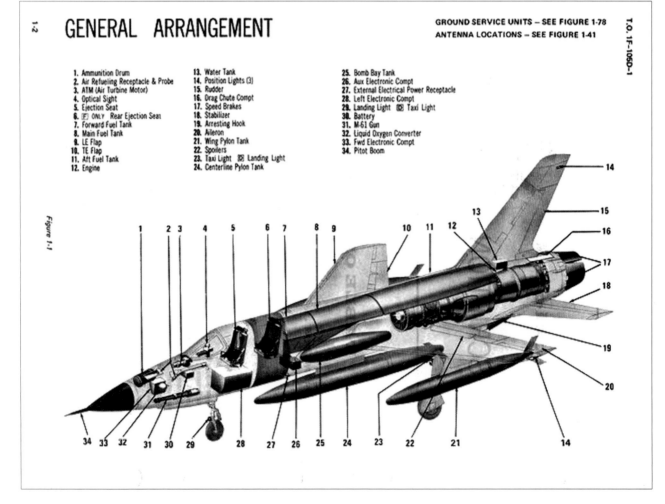

Open 'petals' of the airbrake, and brake parachute hatch. (USAF)

F-105B avionics. (USAF)

Arresting hook scheme. (USAF)

T.O. 1F-105B-2-11

FIRE-CONTROL SYSTEM
Installation

1. RADOME
2. RADAR ANTENNA
3. ACCESS DOOR FF2
4. RADAR-FREQUENCY-CONVERTER TRANSMITTER
5. RADAR MODULATOR
6. ACCESS DOOR FF4
7. PRESSURE REGULATOR
8. DESICCATOR
9. NOSE RELAY BOX
10. KB-3 CAMERA
11. AUTOMATIC-LEAD-COMPUTING SIGHT
12. ACCESS DOOR FF12
13. ROLL-ERROR COMPUTER
14. SIGHT-ELECTRONIC-CONTROL AMPLIFIER
15. TOSS-BOMB COMPUTER
16. RADAR-AMPLIFIER POWER SUPPLY
17. PITCH CONTROL
18. RADAR-RANGE COMPUTER
19. ACCESS DOOR FF17
20. RADAR WAVEGUIDE
21. "CAGING" BUTTON
22. MANUAL RANGE CONTROL
23. "MASTER ARMAMENT" SWITCH
24. "SIGHT" CONTROL
25. "SIGHT SPAN" CONTROL
26. "SIGHT RETICLE" CONTROL
27. "ROLL" INDICATOR
28. "WEAPON RELEASE" LIGHT
29. BOMB-ROCKET BUTTON
30. "TARGET REJECT" SWITCH

31. STICK GRIP BBA
32. "TRIGGER" SWITCH
33. ARMAMENT-CIRCUIT-BREAKER PANEL
34. "BURST HT" CONTROL
35. "IP RANGE" CONTROL
36. "TARGET PRESS" CONTROL
37. "WEAPONS SELECTOR" SWITCH
38. "RANGE WIND" CONTROL
39. "BOMB MODE SEL" SWITCH
40. "CVDA" CONTROL
41. "CAMERA EXPOSURE" SWITCH
42. "ARMAMENT CONTROLS" PANEL
43. "RANGE WIND" SWITCH
44. "FAST ERECT" SWITCH

45. "RADAR RESET" SWITCH
46. DEPRESSION CONTROL

DETAIL A
MA-8 FIRE CONTROL
EQUIPMENT INSTALLATION

DETAIL B
COCKPIT CONTROLS

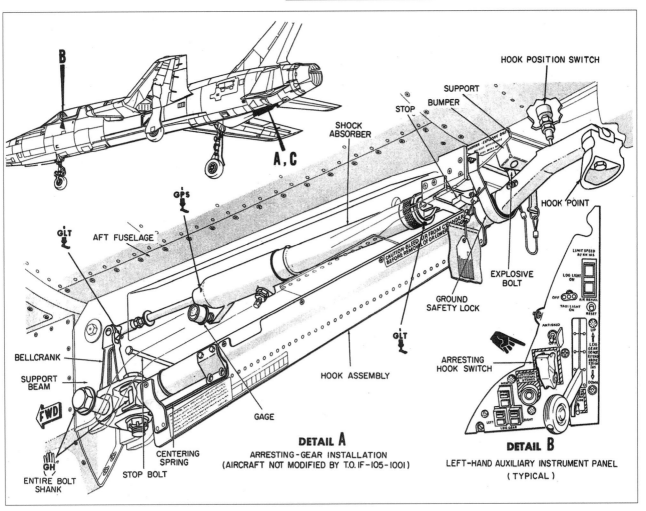

HOOK POSITION SWITCH

SUPPORT

BUMPER

STOP

SHOCK ABSORBER

HOOK POINT

GPS

AFT FUSELAGE

EXPLOSIVE BOLT

GLT

GROUND SAFETY LOCK

GLT

BELLCRANK

SUPPORT BEAM

HOOK ASSEMBLY

ARRESTING HOOK SWITCH

FWD

ENTIRE BOLT SHANK

STOP BOLT

CENTERING SPRING

GAGE

DETAIL A
ARRESTING-GEAR INSTALLATION
(AIRCRAFT NOT MODIFIED BY T.O. IF-105-1001)

DETAIL B
LEFT-HAND AUXILIARY INSTRUMENT PANEL
(TYPICAL)

121

intended for use in emergency landings, allowing the aircraft to engage arresting gear such as the BAK-6 water squeezer, BAK-9 brake system, BAK-12 tape system or MA-1A chain barrier at speeds between 120 and 156 kts (222 – 289 km/h), depending on aircraft weight. A fuselage compartment at the base of the rudder housed a 20ft diameter ring-slot braking parachute that

Both pages: Servicing diagram of aircraft systems. (USAF)

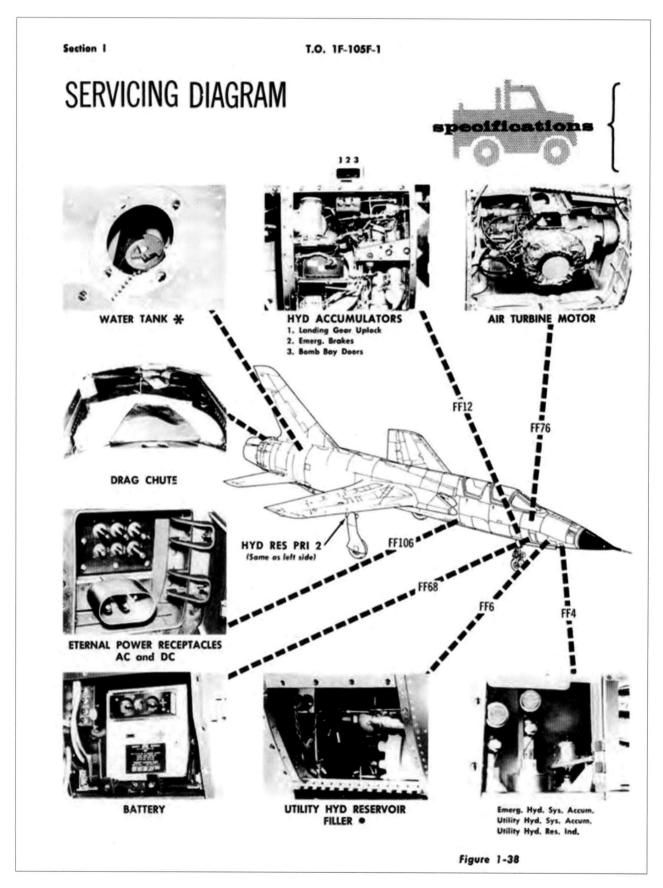

Section I   T.O. 1F-105F-1

SERVICING DIAGRAM

specifications

WATER TANK ✳

HYD ACCUMULATORS
1. Landing Gear Uplock
2. Emerg. Brakes
3. Bomb Bay Doors

AIR TURBINE MOTOR

DRAG CHUTE

FF12

FF76

HYD RES PRI 2
(Same as left side)

FF106

FF68

FF6

FF4

ETERNAL POWER RECEPTACLES AC and DC

BATTERY

UTILITY HYD RESERVOIR FILLER ●

Emerg. Hyd. Sys. Accum.
Utility Hyd. Sys. Accum.
Utility Hyd. Res. Ind.

Figure 1-38

was normally released after touchdown. Its position directly above the afterburner sometimes caused heat damage to the parachute, if the afterburner had been heavily used. The limiting speed for brake chute release was 200kts. If the brake chute was deployed above this speed a frangible pin cut it free to prevent aircraft damage.

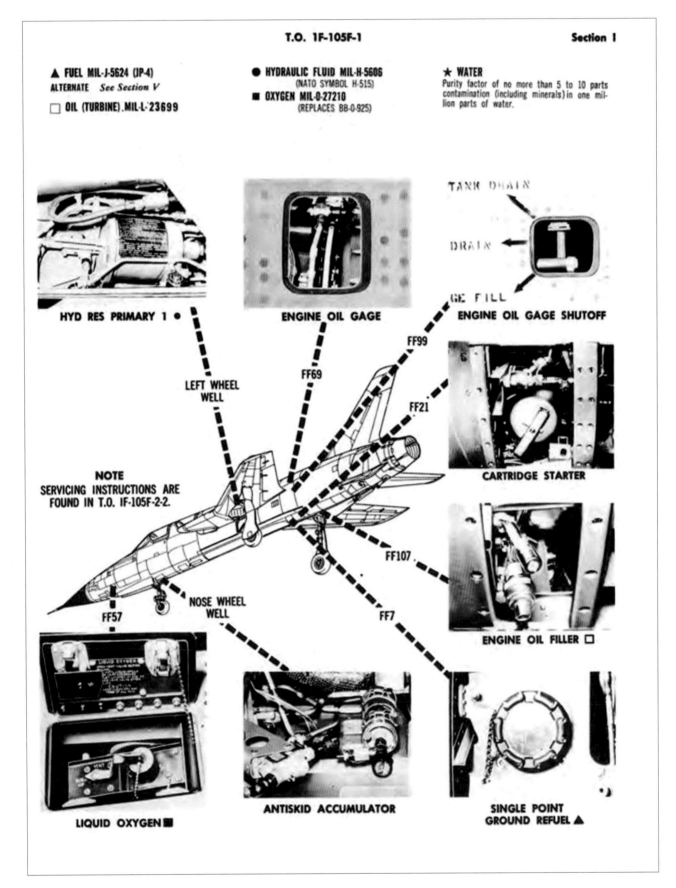

▲ FUEL MIL-J-5624 (JP-4)
ALTERNATE   *See Section V*

☐ OIL (TURBINE) MIL-L-23699

● HYDRAULIC FLUID MIL-H-5606
   (NATO SYMBOL H-515)
■ OXYGEN MIL-O-27210
   (REPLACES BB-O-925)

★ WATER
Purity factor of no more than 5 to 10 parts contamination (including minerals) in one million parts of water.

HYD RES PRIMARY 1 ●

ENGINE OIL GAGE

TANK DRAIN
DRAIN ←
GE FILL

ENGINE OIL GAGE SHUTOFF

FF99

LEFT WHEEL WELL

FF69

FF21

CARTRIDGE STARTER

NOTE
SERVICING INSTRUCTIONS ARE FOUND IN T.O. 1F-105F-2-2.

FF107

ENGINE OIL FILLER ☐

FF57

NOSE WHEEL WELL

FF7

LIQUID OXYGEN ■

ANTISKID ACCUMULATOR

SINGLE POINT GROUND REFUEL ▲

SERVICING DOORS AND PANELS

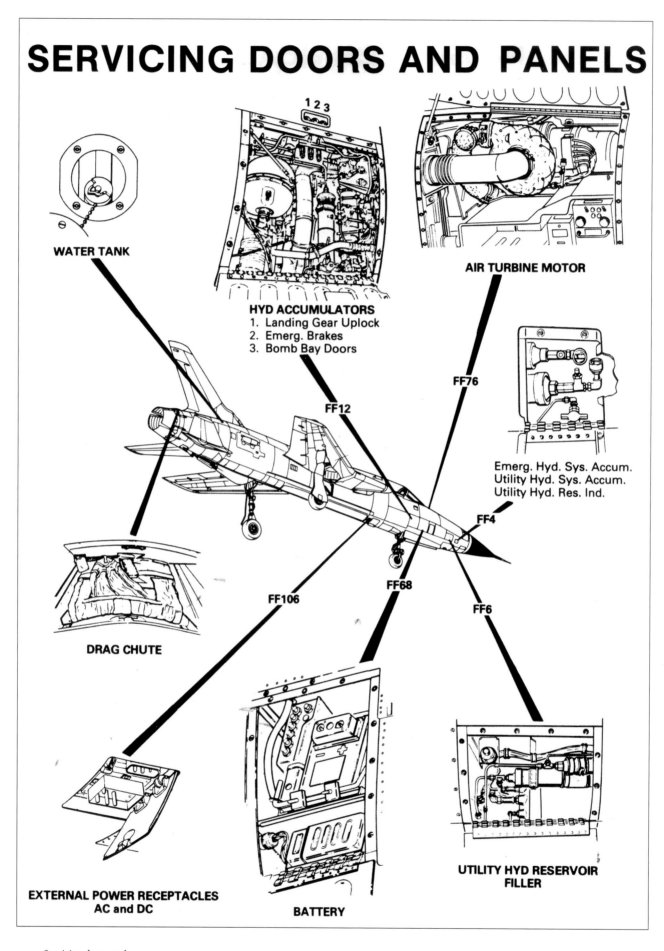

WATER TANK

HYD ACCUMULATORS
1. Landing Gear Uplock
2. Emerg. Brakes
3. Bomb Bay Doors

AIR TURBINE MOTOR

FF76

FF12

Emerg. Hyd. Sys. Accum.
Utility Hyd. Sys. Accum.
Utility Hyd. Res. Ind.

FF4

DRAG CHUTE

FF106

FF68

FF6

**EXTERNAL POWER RECEPTACLES
AC and DC**

BATTERY

**UTILITY HYD RESERVOIR
FILLER**

*Servicing doors and
panels diagram. (USAF)*

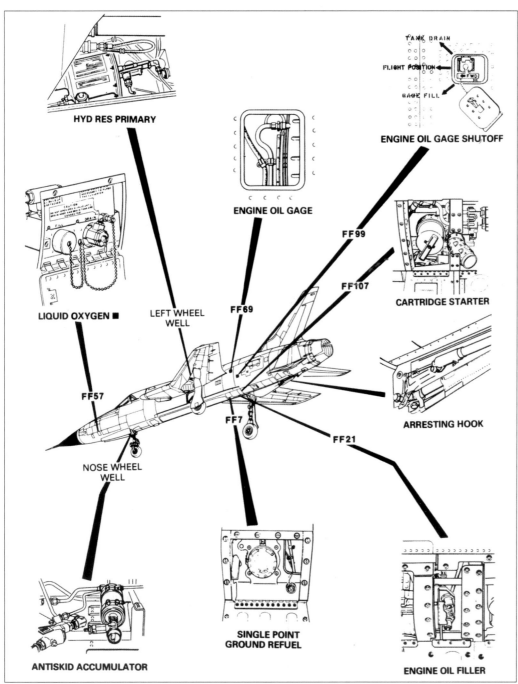

HYD RES PRIMARY

ENGINE OIL GAGE

TANK DRAIN

FLIGHT POSITION ← FWD

GAGE FILL

ENGINE OIL GAGE SHUTOFF

FF99

FF107

CARTRIDGE STARTER

LIQUID OXYGEN ■

LEFT WHEEL WELL

FF69

FF57

FF7

ARRESTING HOOK

NOSE WHEEL WELL

FF21

ANTISKID ACCUMULATOR

SINGLE POINT GROUND REFUEL

ENGINE OIL FILLER

Servicing diagram of aircraft systems. (USAF)

Servicing doors and panels diagram. (USAF)

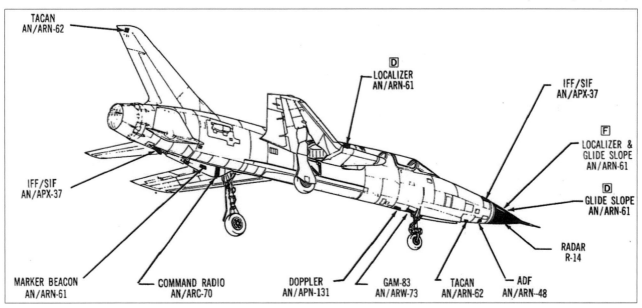

TACAN AN/ARN-62

D
LOCALIZER AN/ARN-61

IFF/SIF AN/APX-37

F
LOCALIZER & GLIDE SLOPE AN/ARN-61

D
GLIDE SLOPE AN/ARN-61

IFF/SIF AN/APX-37

RADAR R-14

MARKER BEACON AN/ARN-61

COMMAND RADIO AN/ARC-70

DOPPLER AN/APN-131

GAM-83 AN/ARW-73

TACAN AN/ARN-62

ADF AN/ARN-48

An F-105D undergoing maintenance. Open panels reveal the ATM and Ram Air Turbine. (USAF)

F-105D-6-RE (59-1822) 'The Polish Glider' from the 44th TFS, 355th TFW preserved at the Polish Aviation Museum, Cracow. (Jarosław Dobrzyński)

Details of the nose landing gear with GCA radar reflector (the nosewheel in the photo is not original, but from a MiG-21). (Jarosław Dobrzyński).

Nose landing gear well. (Jarosław Dobrzyński)

Rear view of F-105D-6-RE (59-1822) 'The Polish Glider' from the 44th TFS, 355th TFW preserved at the Polish Aviation Museum, Cracow. Afterburner cooling scoops are visible. (Jarosław Dobrzyński)

Above, left: Alternator and oil cooler air intake between APR-26 Launch Warning Receiver and VHF antennas. (Jarosław Dobrzyński)

Above, right: Engine bleed air doors, port side. (Jarosław Dobrzyński)

Right: Port rear blue formation light. (Jarosław Dobrzyński)

Port side of the forward fuselage with refuelling receptacle, cannon port, vents and exhaust for the alternator and oil cooler, and forward blue formation light. (Jarosław Dobrzyński)

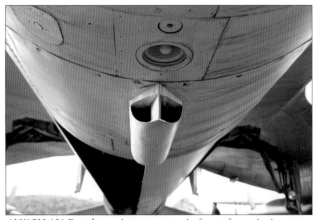

AN/APN-131 Doppler navigator antenna in front of an avionics cooling air intake. (Jarosław Dobrzyński).

Starboard blue formation light, white tail illumination light and brake parachute compartment hatch. (Jarosław Dobrzyński)

Hydraulic pressure gauges, used by ground crew when servicing the hydraulic system, forward blue formation light and ATM exhaust on the starboard side. (Jarosław Dobrzyński)

Starboard afterburner cooling scoop. (Jarosław Dobrzyński)

Angle of attack vane. (Jarosław Dobrzyński)

Upper red anti-collision beacon. (Jarosław Dobrzyński)

APR-25 antenna housing and strike camera under the nose. (Jarosław Dobrzyński)

An F-105D undergoing maintenance at Takhli. Note exposed AN/APR-25 RHAW antenna under the nose. (USAF)

Fuel dump nozzle. (Jarosław Dobrzyński)

Forward red anti-collision beacon. (Jarosław Dobrzyński)

Details of the bomb bay. The bomb rack actuator cylinder in lowered position is visible in the middle. (Jarosław Dobrzyński)

Flare and chaff dispenser on rear lower fuselage. (Jarosław Dobrzyński)

The muzzle of the six-barrel M61A1 Vulcan rotary cannon. (USAF)

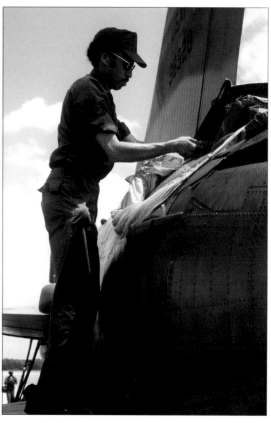

A mechanic loading the brake parachute. (USAF)

Details of the six-barrel M61A1 Vulcan rotary cannon. (Donald Kutyna archive via MLP)

Details of extended refuelling probe. (USAF)

Wing

The wing was centre-mounted, 385 sq.ft (35.7 sq.m) in area, and had a 45° sweep angle and 3° anhedral. The aerofoils used were NACA low-drag types, 65A-005.5 section at the root and 65A-003.7 at the tip (the last digits indicate wing thickness ratio, 5.5 and 3.7 respectively). The wing loading of the F-105D was high, between 120 and 137 lb/sq.ft (585 – 669 kg/sq.m). The wing had two main aluminum spars running the full length, with another single structure at right angles to the centreline. At the wing roots forward-swept variable-geometry (VAI) air intakes were mounted. Conventional ailerons were incorporated in the wing. They were used only at subsonic speeds, working in conjunction with five powered spoilers above each wing. For roll control at higher speeds only the spoilers were used. Fowler flaps that could be lowered

Details of the starboard air intake. (Jarosław Dobrzyński)

450 US gal underwing tank. (Jarosław Dobrzyński)

to 34.5° were mounted on the trailing edges and full-span leading edge flaps (lowering up to 20°) for takeoff and landing, and to add lift when the aircraft was manoeuvring, were fitted. For take-off and landing both flaps were used at full deflection. For subsonic cruising and manoeuvring only the leading edge flaps were employed.

The trailing-edge flaps could also be used individually to provide roll control if the vertical tailplane was damaged.

The wings included the main landing gear wells with auxiliary air intakes, covered with a mesh grid, used for engine ground run-ups and taxiing. The inwards-retracting landing gear struts were very long, to provide ground clearance for weapon loads and the ventral fin. The wheels had hydraulic brakes with antiskid units.

Details of the port and the starboard air intake. (Jarosław Dobrzyński)

Details of the starboard main landing gear. (Jarosław Dobrzyński)

Port and starboard landing gear well. Note circular auxiliary engine air intake, covered with mesh grille. (Jarosław Dobrzyński)

Flight control system

The flight control surfaces were operated by hydraulic actuators, linked to the pilot's control column by push-pull rods and cables. An artificial feel device to simulate the effects of airflow on the control surfaces at different speeds was also linked to the pilot's control column and rudder pedals.

The F-105D/F was fitted with the AF/A42G12 Automatic Flight Control System that had three basic modes of operation:

Stability Augmentation, helping the pilot to maintain straight and level flight by damping oscillations about the pitch and yaw axes.

Autopilot with following submodes: Altitude hold; Mach hold; NAV/Track hold

Fully automatic modes of Instrument Landing System approach and AUTOSS (automatic Toss-Bomb) manoeuvre.

The controls were located on a single panel on the left console in each cockpit and an AFCS emergency disconnect lever on the control stick permitted disengagement of all AFCS modes.

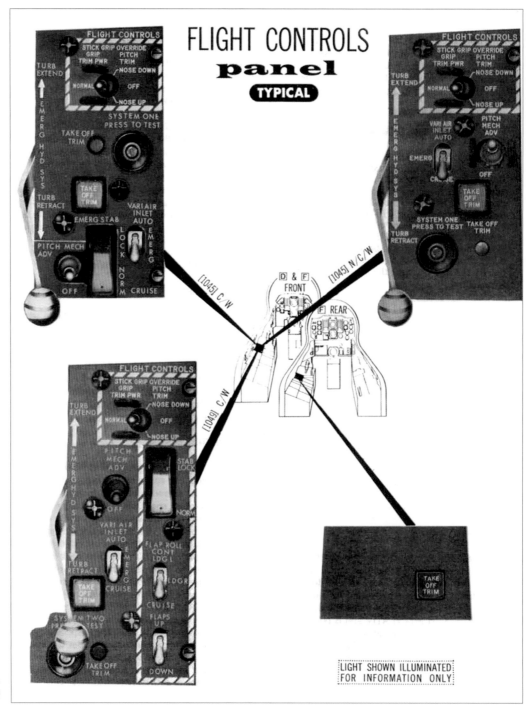

Flight control panels.
(USAF)

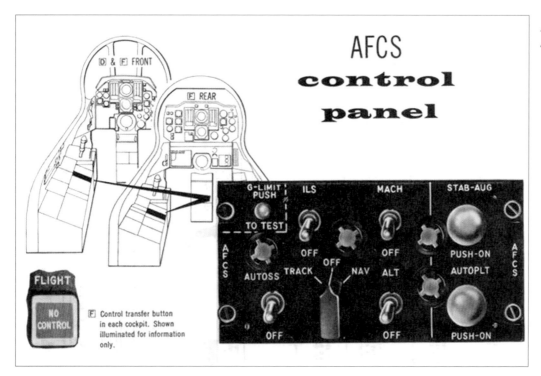

Automatic Flight Control System panel. (USAF)

Hydraulic system

The F-105 had three separate hydraulic systems: the utility system, primary 1 and primary 2 systems. The utility system provided for the aircraft's nose-wheel steering, landing gear, brakes and speed brakes, flaps, air intake control, and M61 cannon drive mechanism. The parallel primary 1 and primary 2 systems controlled the spoilers, ailerons, stabilator, and rudder for the port and starboard sides of the aircraft respectively. All systems had their own hydraulic reservoirs, engine-driven pumps, and fluid lines running at a maximum pressure of 3,000 psi (20,684 kPa). In case of engine failure the emergency ram-air turbine (RAT) could be extended for limited flight control via the primary 1 system.

The hydraulic systems were the Achilles' heel of the F-105 because their lines ran close to each other in the aircraft's belly and were not protected against flak damage, as this wasn't thought necessary for the aircraft's original nuclear strike mission. However, in combat over Vietnam the hydraulic lines were frequently damaged by enemy fire, which resulted in rapid loss of hydraulic pressure, making the F-105 uncontrollable. The damaged systems forced the tailplane into a position that caused a steep dive as the pressure dropped. From 1967 most F-105s were retrofitted with a lock operated by the pilot's 'Emerg[ency]. Stab[ilator].' switch, fixing the stabilator in the neutral position and transferring control authority to emergency pitch and roll switches and the trailing edge flaps. This often enabled a damaged aircraft to stay aloft a little longer so that the pilot could reach a safer bail-out area. A later modification added a fourth hydraulic reservoir and a set of hydraulic lines in an extra fairing in the fuselage spine, which were powered by the RAT and enabled limited use of the tail flight control surfaces, and the landing gear to be extended.

Powerplant

The F-105D and F were powered by the Pratt & Whitney J75-P-19W two-spool axial-flow turbojet, rated at 16,100 lb (71.6 kN) at sea level, 24,500 lb (108.9 kN) with afterburner and 26,500 lb (117.87 kn) for a one-minute take-off boost with water injection engaged. This extra power was almost always necessary for heavy weight combat take-offs in the hot and humid conditions of South-East Asia. The water injection was engaged by a switch near the throttle and the water was sprayed at 110 psi (758 kPa) ahead of the first compressor stage. If the water injection was not used, the water was automatically dumped, because the 136-litre (36-gallon) water tank was not stressed for flight. There was interconnection between the cockpit pressurisation system and the water tank, so that when the cockpit was pressurised, the water was automatically purged. This meant that the pilots had to remember not to pressurise the cockpit before take-off. Dumping water before take-off resulted in a mission abort, so the pilots had to withstand heat before take-off, because only when airborne could the cockpit be pressurised and the air conditioning system engaged.

The engine had an eight-stage low pressure compressor, seven-stage high pressure compressor, eight-stage 'cannular' combustion chamber (combustion 'cans' within a common annulus), a split three-stage turbine and afterburner with two-position nozzle. The engine was started by cartridge pneumatic system or compressed air. In permanent Stateside bases, a compressed air start was usually used, but in combat conditions during the war, the cartridge start was used as a quicker method.

In combat conditions, when engines ran at maximum military power and afterburner for extended periods of time, their durability was shorter than anticipated, which resulted in failures. This problem was not realised for a long time, as when it happened in flight, over hostile territory, it tended to be attributed to enemy fire. The crash of 1st Lt Joseph Vojir of 421st TFS in F-105D (62-4312) due to engine failure on take-off at Korat on 18 July 1966 (the pilot ejected and survived) revealed heat fatigue cracks in turbine blades. It was realised that the engines' Time Between Overhaul must be reduced to avoid failures. Special multipliers were developed for calculation of engine wear in combat missions. For easier and shorter missions to Laos and Route Pack 1 the engine running time was multiplied by 1.5, and for toughest missions to Route Pack 6, by 5.

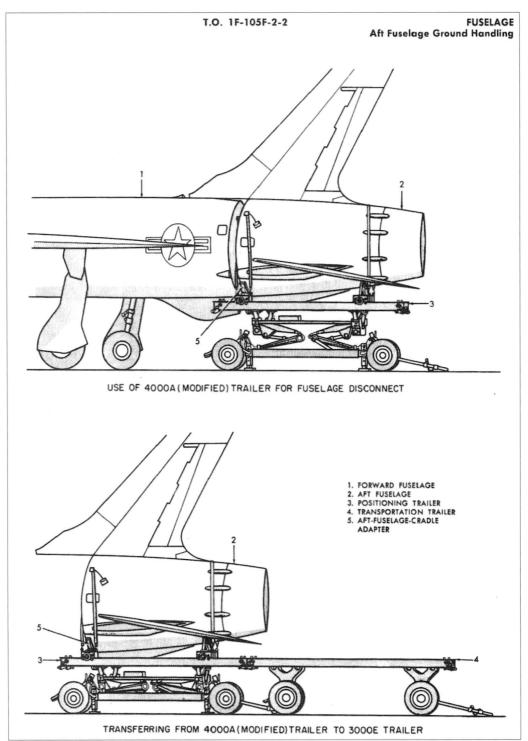

Fuselage disconnect scheme. (USAF)

ENGINE J-75

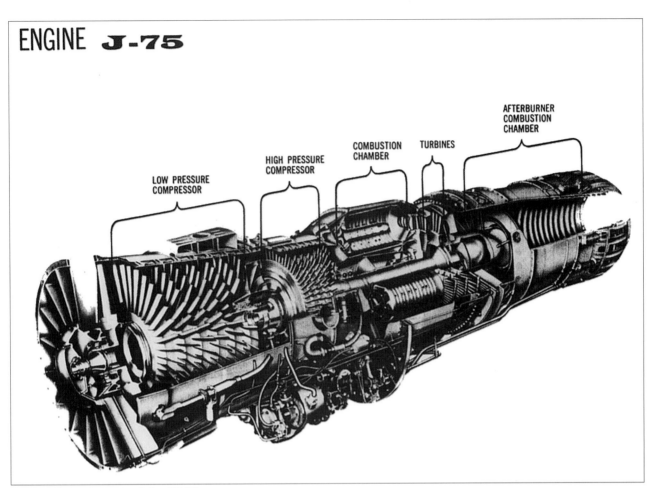

LOW PRESSURE
COMPRESSOR

HIGH PRESSURE
COMPRESSOR

COMBUSTION
CHAMBER

TURBINES

AFTERBURNER
COMBUSTION
CHAMBER

Pratt & Whitney J75-P-19 turbojet. (USAF)

Details of the afterburner. (Donald Kutyna archive via MLP)

Mechanics install an overhauled engine in an F-105D at Takhli. (USAF

Engine maintenance of an F-105D at Takhli. Note the detached tail section on a special trolley. (USAF)

Fuel system

The F-105D/F had three internal bladder fuel tanks in the fuselage, of total capacity 4,391 litres (1,051 US gals). The aft tank was wrapped around the upper part of the engine, which could be dangerous, as turbine failure could rupture this tank, resulting in fire. The F-105's fuel consumption was very high, so provisions for several additional tanks were made. A 390 US gal (1,476 l) non-jettisonable fuel tank could be mounted in the internal bomb bay and either a 450 US gal (1,703 l) or 650 US gal (2,460 l) external tank could be carried on the fuselage centreline pylon. Two 450-gal tanks with integral pylons could be carried on the inboard wing stores attachment points. The maximum fuel supply was 2,976 US gal (11,265 l), weighing 19,344 lb (8,774 kg).

The F-105 was fitted with two in-flight refuelling systems. Initially only the probe-and-drogue method was used, and a retractable probe was mounted on the upper port side of the forward fuselage, just ahead of the cockpit. Later, when the USAF adopted the flying boom refuelling method, a receptacle with hydraulically-operated drop-down door was added in the upper nose area, ahead of the probe, and this was retrofitted to earlier aircraft. During the Vietnam War both methods of refuelling were used, depending on the available tanker's equipment, although the flying boom method was more common, and less experienced pilots sometimes had difficulties using the other system, which they often had to learn in combat conditions.

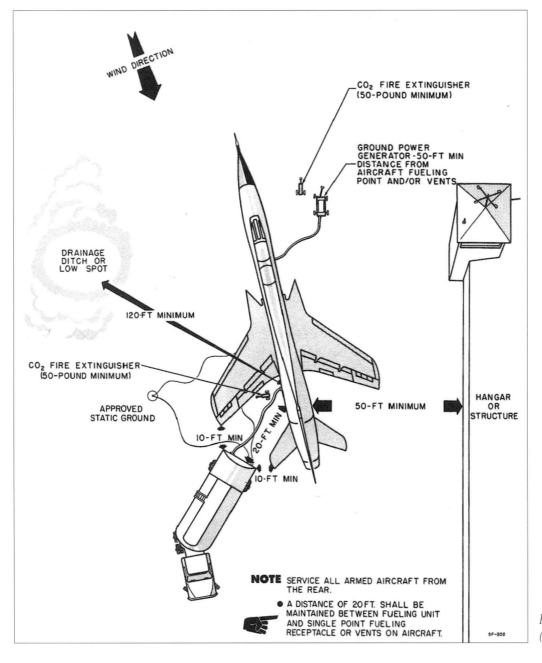

Refuelling instruction.
(USAF)

FUEL QUANTITY
data

DATA DATE: MAY 1963

DATA BASIS: ESTIMATED

U.S. GALLONS AND POUNDS

POUNDS SHOWN ARE FOR STANDARD DAY CONDITIONS ONLY AND ARE BASED ON 6.5 POUNDS PER GALLON OF JP-4 FUEL. FOR MORE PRECISE ACCURACY THE WEIGHT OF FUEL SHOULD BE SAMPLED AT THE LOCAL ENVIRONMENT.

		USABLE FUEL		FULLY SERVICED	
		GALS	POUNDS	GALS	POUNDS
CENTERLINE PYLON	450 GAL TANK	450.0	2925.0	452.5	2941.0
	650 GAL TANK	650.0	4225.0	653.0	4244.5
	LEFT INBOARD PYLON TANK	450.0	2925.0	452.5	2941.0
	RIGHT INBOARD PYLON TANK	450.0	2925.0	452.5	2941.0
	BOMB BAY TANK	390.0	2535.0	391.0	2541.5
	MAIN TANK*	1135.0	7377.5	1148.0	7467.0
	FUEL IN LINES	25.0	162.5	25.0	162.5
	FWD TANK	376.0	2444.0	380.0	2470.0
	MAIN TANK	257.0	1670.5	260.0	1690.0
	AFT TANK	502.0	3263.0	508.0	3302.0

*MAIN TANK FUEL IS OBTAINED FROM THREE INTERNAL TANKS

	USABLE FUEL	
	GALS	POUNDS
MAXIMUM INTERNAL FUEL WITHOUT BOMB BAY TANK	1160.0	7540.0
MAX INT FUEL WITH B/B TANK AND THREE 450 GAL EXT TANKS	2900.0	18850.0
MAX INT FUEL WITH B/B TANK AND TWO 450 AND ONE 650 EXT TANKS	3100.0	20150.0

390 US gal bomb bay tank in lowered position. (USAF)

Cockpit

The cockpit was quite spacious, heated and air-conditioned by a Hamilton Standard system drawing bleed air from the engine. Oxygen in both F-105D and F variants was supplied from a 10-litre bottle mounted in the nose. The pilot sat on a Republic ejection seat with armour-plated headrest and electrical height adjustment. The seat included a Koch fibreglass box containing a survival kit and dinghy, and an MC-1 rubber seat cushion. The force-deployed parachute was worn on the pilot's back and formed the seat back cushion. In ejections above 15,500 ft, parachute opening was delayed to allow the pilot to fall to a more oxygen-rich atmosphere, and in ejections at low altitude a zero-delay lanyard was attached to deploy the parachute right after the pilot separated from the seat. To assist separation, hinged drag plates extended at both sides of the headrest. The ejection was initiated by pulling on two yellow handles on either side of the seat base, which tightened the pilot's harness and leg restraints. A further squeeze of the trigger set into the handles jettisoned the canopy and fired the seat. In two-seat variants, the ejection could be initiated from both cockpits, but the rear seat ejected first.

The F-105B instrument panel had traditional circular, clock-type instruments. The F-105D/F instrument panel had an innovative design with four instruments making an integrated instrument system. At the top was the attitude director indicator (ADI), displaying roll and pitch attitude, turn and slip rates, computing bank steering information, glide slope displacement for instrument landings, and bank and pitch information to intercept and follow the glide slope and localiser beams. Below it was the horizontal situation indicator (HSI) that displayed magnetic heading, bearing, command heading, information about course and displacement from the course, to-from indication and distance from desired TACAN station, target or destination. Below the HSI the radar display was located.

Two new instruments were located on either side of the ADI and HSI. They were rectangular in shape and used vertical bars indicating key information, supplemented by additional data on the faces. Flight information was presented by means of movable lines related to fixed reference lines, set by the pilot. On the left the Airspeed Mach Indicator (AMI) was located. It presented safe speed warnings, calibrated airspeed, true Mach number and vertical G loads. On the right the Altitude and Vertical Velocity Indicator was located. It displayed the vertical velocity (rate of climb or descent), pressure altitude, and altitudes of the aircraft and target.

F-105D cockpit. Note the RHAW scope right to the sight. (USAF)

Engine and hydraulic instruments were located on the right side of the main panel, and on the left side were auxiliary flight instruments and armament controls. Below the radar scope was a special weapons control panel.

On the left console were located the throttle quadrant with water injection switch, air start button, flap lever and position indicator, radar, toss-bomb computer, AFCS and command radio control panels, cockpit utility light and pilot relief container. The right console was home to the armament jettison buttons, cartridge starter switch and AN/APN-131 Doppler navigation system, AN/ARN-62 TACAN, AN/ARN-61 ILS and optional LORAN system control panels.

Opposite page: F-105D cockpit. Note the RHAW scope right to the sight. (USAF)

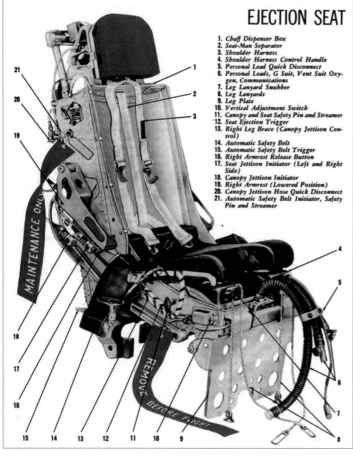

EJECTION SEAT

1. Chaff Dispenser Box
2. Seat-Man Separator
3. Shoulder Harness
4. Shoulder Harness Control Handle
5. Personal Lead Quick Disconnect
6. Personal Leads, G Suit, Vent Suit Oxygen, Communications
7. Leg Lanyard Snubber
8. Leg Lanyards
9. Leg Plate
10. Vertical Adjustment Switch
11. Canopy and Seat Safety Pin and Streamer
12. Seat Ejection Trigger
13. Right Leg Brace (Canopy Jettison Control)
14. Automatic Safety Belt
15. Automatic Safety Belt Trigger
16. Right Armrest Release Button
17. Seat Jettison Initiator (Left and Right Side)
18. Canopy Jettison Initiator
19. Right Armrest (Lowered Position)
20. Canopy Jettison Hose Quick Disconnect
21. Automatic Safety Belt Initiator, Safety Pin and Streamer

F-105 ejection seat. (USAF)

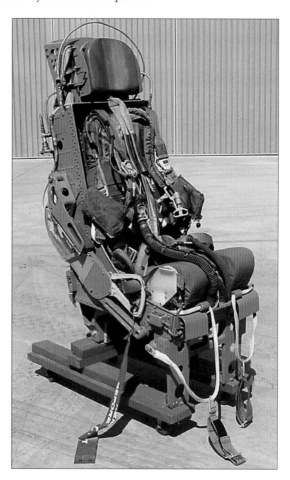

F-105 ejection seat with parachute. (USAF)

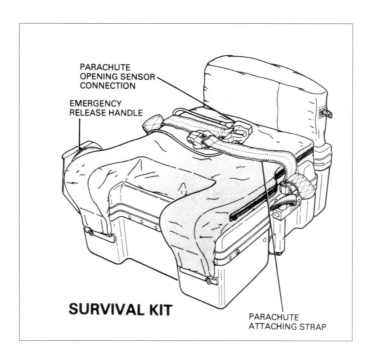

PARACHUTE OPENING SENSOR CONNECTION

EMERGENCY RELEASE HANDLE

SURVIVAL KIT

PARACHUTE ATTACHING STRAP

Avionics, Communications, Identification and Navigation System

The F-105D/F, as an aircraft intended for delivering nuclear strikes deep into enemy territory, was fitted with a then-state-of-the-art navigation system, enabling the finding of distant targets and precise ordnance delivery. It was basically an inertial analogue computer system with three axis accelerometers, with ground speed input from a Doppler radar aimed forward, which transmitted three beams of microwave energy to the ground through three antenna horns, and received the ground reflected energy (echoes). The frequency of the received signal was compared to the frequency of the transmitted signal. The difference in frequency for each beam was resolved into north-south and east-west velocity, which was used to compute ground track, drift and ground speed.

The AN/APN-131 Doppler Navigation System was an automatic, self-contained navigator with associated controls and indicators that showed direction and distance to fly from present position to a selected destination. It was integrated with other aircraft systems: the all-attitude compass system for heading information, air-data computer for true airspeed, the attitude director for steering information. The navigation data was indicated on the HSI. The desired destination could be entered as latitude and longitude by two slewing levers on the control panel on the right console, and a pointer moving around the compass card of this gauge would point directly to the target. There was also a second pointer of a different colour that would point to radio transmissions received. The target pointer was also supported by a mileage calculation shown in an odometer-like window. This could also be selected to TACAN radio

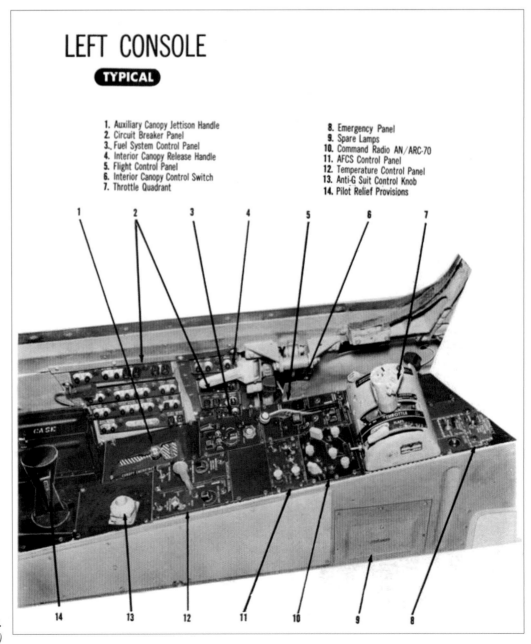

F-105B left console.
(USAF)

beacons, giving bearing and distance. A large gauge on the right side of the panel indicated exact Doppler radar ground speed and a wind drift angle pointer.

The Doppler navigator linked to the automatic pilot to provide automatic navigation to the pre-set destination and with the fire control system to provide track-hold during the bombing modes.

In flight the computer had to be updated by syncing to a TACAN/DME by using two (computed position) slewing levers, to make the angle and computed distance of the computer location agree with the bearing needle & DME indicator in the panel.

During long-range combat missions over North Vietnam the AN/APN-131 was the most important navigation device. As Ed Rasimus explained: "*The Doppler was a go/no go item. If your Doppler was out, your aeroplane was out. Knowing how to use it, how to update it and what its capabilities were was basic*"[1].

Other components of the AN/ASQ-37 CIN (Communications, Identification and Navigation) system were the AN/ARC-70 UHF command set for long-range voice transmission, the AN/ARA-48 Direction Finder, finding 225 to 400 MHz transmitters within range, AN/ARN-61 instrument landing system with glide-slope, localiser, marker beacon and visual-aural indications, AN/ARN-62 TACAN (Tactical Air Navigation) system with range and bearing information, and AN/APX-27 identification radar system providing identification data for IFF interrogation

---

1   Davies, Peter, E., *F-105 Thunderchief Units of the Vietnam War*, Osprey Publishing 2010, p.8.

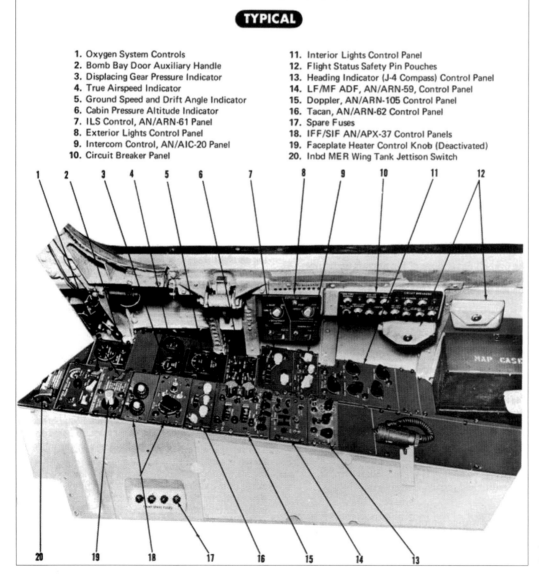

RIGHT CONSOLE

TYPICAL

1. Oxygen System Controls
2. Bomb Bay Door Auxiliary Handle
3. Displacing Gear Pressure Indicator
4. True Airspeed Indicator
5. Ground Speed and Drift Angle Indicator
6. Cabin Pressure Altitude Indicator
7. ILS Control, AN/ARN-61 Panel
8. Exterior Lights Control Panel
9. Intercom Control, AN/AIC-20 Panel
10. Circuit Breaker Panel

11. Interior Lights Control Panel
12. Flight Status Safety Pin Pouches
13. Heading Indicator (J-4 Compass) Control Panel
14. LF/MF ADF, AN/ARN-59, Control Panel
15. Doppler, AN/ARN-105 Control Panel
16. Tacan, AN/ARN-62 Control Panel
17. Spare Fuses
18. IFF/SIF AN/APX-37 Control Panels
19. Faceplate Heater Control Knob (Deactivated)
20. Inbd MER Wing Tank Jettison Switch

F-105B right console.
(USAF)

MAIN INSTRUMENT PANEL F & D front

TYPICAL

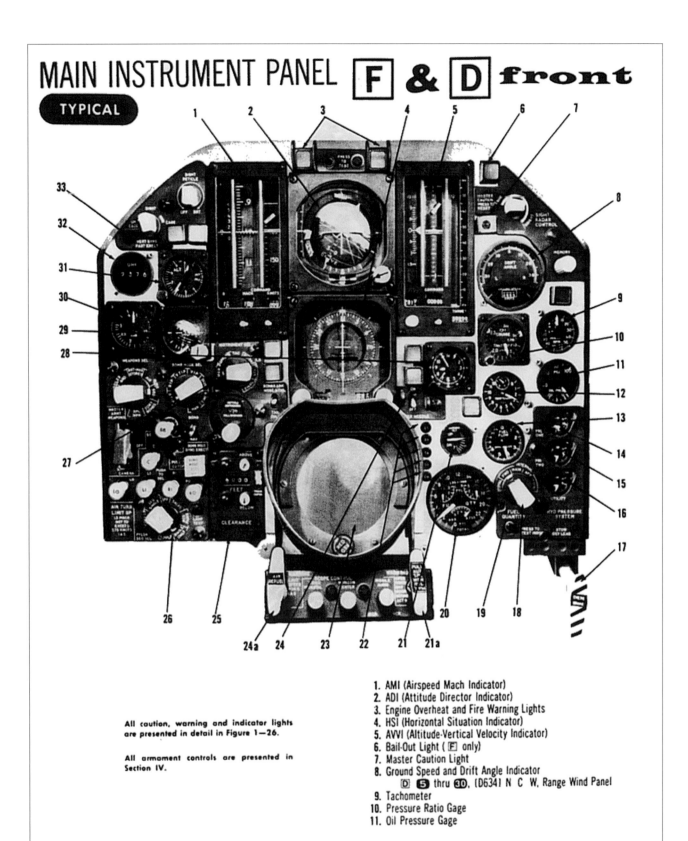

All caution, warning and indicator lights
are presented in detail in Figure 1—26.

All armament controls are presented in
Section IV.

1. AMI (Airspeed Mach Indicator)
2. ADI (Attitude Director Indicator)
3. Engine Overheat and Fire Warning Lights
4. HSI (Horizontal Situation Indicator)
5. AVVI (Altitude-Vertical Velocity Indicator)
6. Bail-Out Light (F only)
7. Master Caution Light
8. Ground Speed and Drift Angle Indicator
     D 5 thru 30, [D634] N C W, Range Wind Panel
9. Tachometer
10. Pressure Ratio Gage
11. Oil Pressure Gage

*Integrated flight
instrument system
scheme. (USAF)*

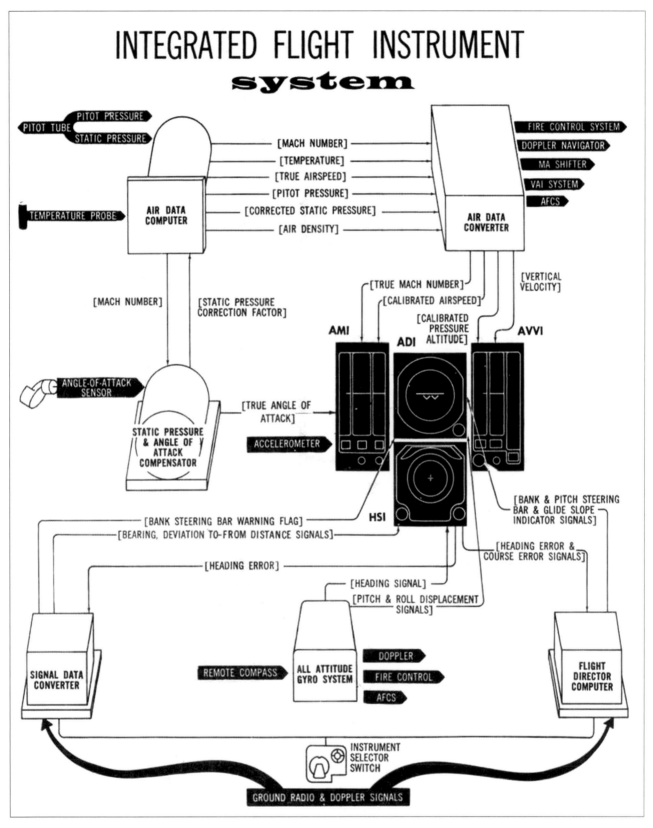

Integrated flight instrument display scheme. (USAF)

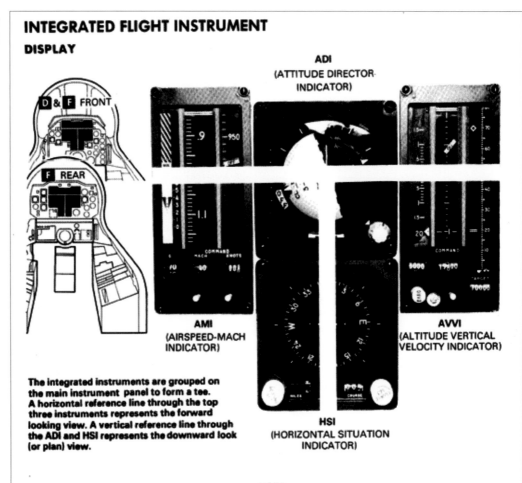

INTEGRATED FLIGHT INSTRUMENT
DISPLAY

D & F FRONT

F REAR

ADI
(ATTITUDE DIRECTOR
INDICATOR)

AMI
(AIRSPEED-MACH
INDICATOR)

AVVI
(ALTITUDE VERTICAL
VELOCITY INDICATOR)

HSI
(HORIZONTAL SITUATION
INDICATOR)

The integrated instruments are grouped on
the main instrument panel to form a tee.
A horizontal reference line through the top
three instruments represents the forward
looking view. A vertical reference line through
the ADI and HSI represents the downward look
(or plan) view.

NOTE

- The display in the forward looking view, along the horizontal reference line,
  is governed by fore and aft movements of the stick and/or throttle, and
  include pitch, airspeed, Mach number, vertical velocity, altitude, angle of
  attack and acceleration.
- The downward looking display is controlled by motions of the stick sideways
  and include heading, bank, turn rate, and navigational as well as tactical
  information.
- By scanning the horizontal or vertical reference lines, it is possible to determine as indicated by the command marker and other indicators whether or
  not the aircraft's performance, in relation to airspeed, altitude, and course,
  differs from the desired performance.

1-F105D-1-69

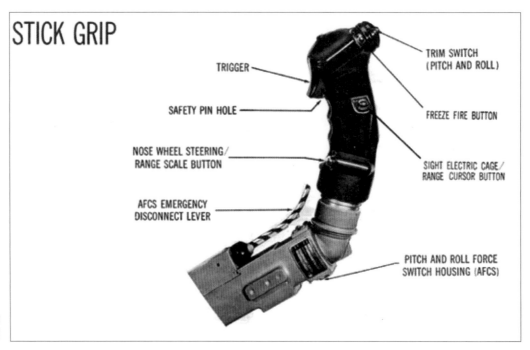

STICK GRIP

TRIGGER

SAFETY PIN HOLE

NOSE WHEEL STEERING/
RANGE SCALE BUTTON

AFCS EMERGENCY
DISCONNECT LEVER

TRIM SWITCH
(PITCH AND ROLL)

FREEZE FIRE BUTTON

SIGHT ELECTRIC CAGE/
RANGE CURSOR BUTTON

PITCH AND ROLL FORCE
SWITCH HOUSING (AFCS)

D and F front

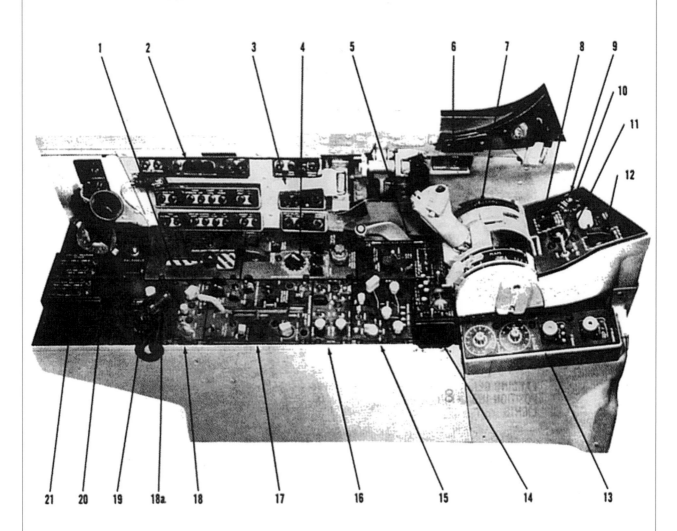

1. Auxiliary Canopy Jettison Handle
2. Circuit Breaker Panel
3. Canopy Lock Lever
4. Fuel System Control Panel
5. Flight Control Panel
6. Interior Canopy Control Switch

7. Throttle Quadrant
8. Emergency Fuel System Switch
9. Flap Position Indicator
10. Air Start Button
11. Water Injection Switch
12. Bail-Out Light Switch (F Only)

13. Toss Bomb Computer Controls
14. Radar, R-14, Control Panel
15. Command Radio, AN, ARC-70, Control Panel
16. AFCS Control Panel
17. Temperature Control Panel
18. Interphone, AN, AIC-20, Control Panel
18a. Cockpit Utility Light F |890| C. W

19. Anti-G Suit Valve Test Button
20. Pilot's Relief Container
21. Special Weapons Circuit Breaker Panel

NOTE

F ONLY, items 20 and 21 are interchanged.

*Left console of F-105F
rear cockpit. (USAF)*

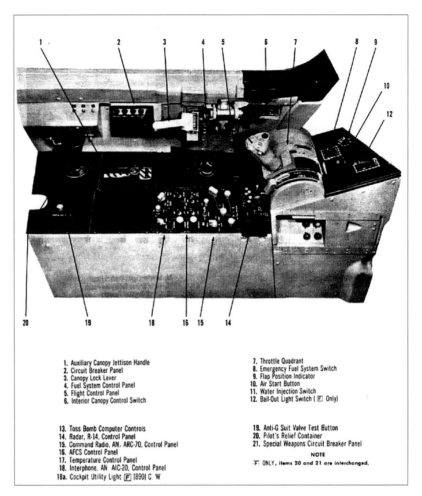

Left console of F-105D cockpit. (USAF)

1. Auxiliary Canopy Jettison Handle
2. Circuit Breaker Panel
3. Canopy Lock Lever
4. Fuel System Control Panel
5. Flight Control Panel
6. Interior Canopy Control Switch

7. Throttle Quadrant
8. Emergency Fuel System Switch
9. Flap Position Indicator
10. Air Start Button
11. Water Injection Switch
12. Bail-Out Light Switch (F Only)

13. Toss Bomb Computer Controls
14. Radar, R-14, Control Panel
15. Command Radio, AN/ARC-70, Control Panel
16. AFCS Control Panel
17. Temperature Control Panel
18. Interphone, AN/AIC-20, Control Panel
18a. Cockpit Utility Light F [890] C/W

19. Anti-G Suit Valve Test Button
20. Pilot's Relief Container
21. Special Weapons Circuit Breaker Panel

NOTE

F ONLY, items 20 and 21 are interchanged.

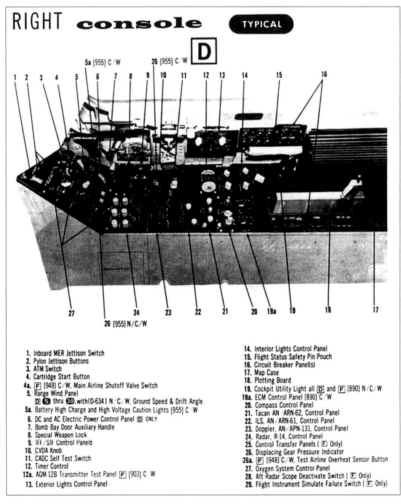

RIGHT console TYPICAL D

1. Inboard MER Jettison Switch
2. Pylon Jettison Buttons
3. ATM Switch
4. Cartridge Start Button
4a. F [948] C/W, Main Airline Shutoff Valve Switch
5. Range Wind Panel
   D 5 thru 30 with [D-634] N/C/W, Ground Speed & Drift Angle.
5a. Battery High Charge and High Voltage Caution Lights [955] C/W
6. DC and AC Electric Power Control Panel D ONLY
7. Bomb Bay Door Auxiliary Handle
8. Special Weapon Lock
9. IFF/SIF Control Panels
10. CVDA Knob
11. CADC Self Test Switch
12. Timer Control
12a. AGM-12B Transmitter Test Panel F [903] C/W
13. Exterior Lights Control Panel

14. Interior Lights Control Panel
15. Flight Status Safety Pin Pouch
16. Circuit Breaker Panel(s)
17. Map Case
18. Plotting Board
19. Cockpit Utility Light all D and F [890] N/C/W
19a. ECM Control Panel [890] C/W
20. Compass Control Panel
21. Tacan AN/ARN-62, Control Panel
22. ILS, AN/ARN-61, Control Panel
23. Doppler, AN/APN-131, Control Panel
24. Radar, R-14, Control Panel
25. Control Transfer Panels (F Only)
26. Displacing Gear Pressure Indicator
26a. F [948] C/W, Test Airline Overheat Sensor Button
27. Oxygen System Control
28. Aft Radar Scope Deactivate Switch (F Only)
29. Flight Instrument Simulate Failure Switch (F Only)

Right console of F-105D cockpit. (USAF)

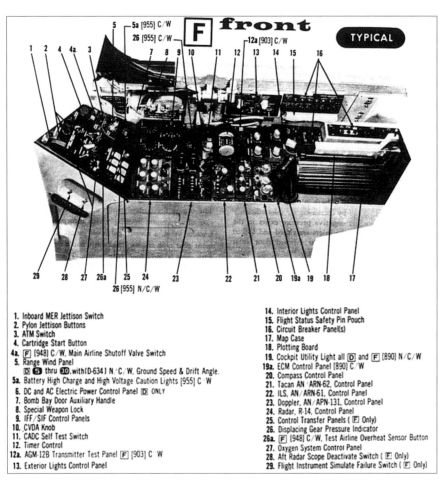

F *front*

TYPICAL

1. Inboard MER Jettison Switch
2. Pylon Jettison Buttons
3. ATM Switch
4. Cartridge Start Button
4a. [F] [948] C/W, Main Airline Shutoff Valve Switch
5. Range Wind Panel
[D] [5] thru [10], with [D-634] N/C/W, Ground Speed & Drift Angle.
5a. Battery High Charge and High Voltage Caution Lights [955] C/W
6. DC and AC Electric Power Control Panel [D] ONLY
7. Bomb Bay Door Auxiliary Handle
8. Special Weapon Lock
9. IFF/SIF Control Panels
10. CVDA Knob
11. CADC Self Test Switch
12. Timer Control
12a. AGM-12B Transmitter Test Panel [F] [903] C/W
13. Exterior Lights Control Panel

14. Interior Lights Control Panel
15. Flight Status Safety Pin Pouch
16. Circuit Breaker Panel(s)
17. Map Case
18. Plotting Board
19. Cockpit Utility Light all [D] and [F] [890] N/C/W
19a. ECM Control Panel [890] C/W
20. Compass Control Panel
21. Tacan AN/ARN-62, Control Panel
22. ILS, AN/ARN-61, Control Panel
23. Doppler, AN/APN-131, Control Panel
24. Radar, R-14, Control Panel
25. Control Transfer Panels ([F] Only)
26. Displacing Gear Pressure Indicator
26a. [F] [948] C/W, Test Airline Overheat Sensor Button
27. Oxygen System Control Panel
28. Aft Radar Scope Deactivate Switch ([F] Only)
29. Flight Instrument Simulate Failure Switch ([F] Only)

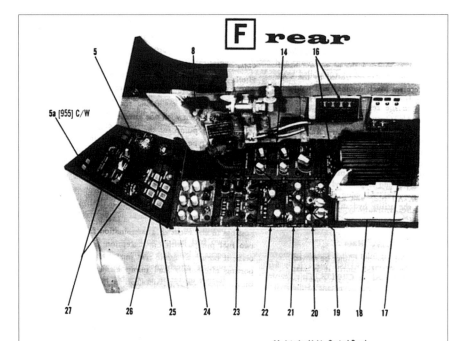

F *rear*

1. Inboard MER Jettison Switch
2. Pylon Jettison Buttons
3. ATM Switch
4. Cartridge Start Button
4a. [F] [948] C/W, Main Airline Shutoff Valve Switch
5. Range Wind Panel
[D] [5] thru [10], with [D-634] N/C/W, Ground Speed & Drift Angle.
5a. Battery High Charge and High Voltage Caution Lights [955] C/W
6. DC and AC Electric Power Control Panel [D] ONLY
7. Bomb Bay Door Auxiliary Handle
8. Special Weapon Lock
9. IFF/SIF Control Panels
10. CVDA Knob
11. CADC Self Test Switch
12. Timer Control
12a. AGM-12B Transmitter Test Panel [F] [903] C/W
13. Exterior Lights Control Panel

14. Interior Lights Control Panel
15. Flight Status Safety Pin Pouch
16. Circuit Breaker Panel(s)
17. Map Case
18. Plotting Board
19. Cockpit Utility Light all [D] and [F] [890] N/C/W
19a. ECM Control Panel [890] C/W
20. Compass Control Panel
21. Tacan AN/ARN-62, Control Panel
22. ILS, AN/ARN-61, Control Panel
23. Doppler, AN/APN-131, Control Panel
24. Radar, R-14, Control Panel
25. Control Transfer Panels ([F] Only)
26. Displacing Gear Pressure Indicator
26a. [F] [948] C/W, Test Airline Overheat Sensor Button
27. Oxygen System Control Panel
28. Aft Radar Scope Deactivate Switch ([F] Only)
29. Flight Instrument Simulate Failure Switch ([F] Only)

Right console of F-105F rear cockpit. (USAF)

151

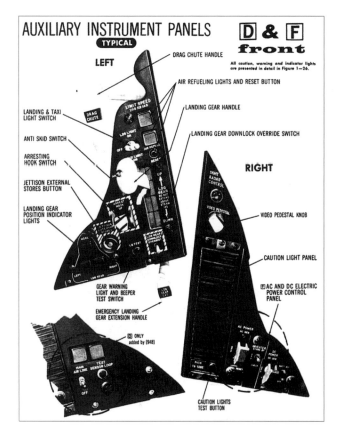

AUXILIARY INSTRUMENT PANELS
TYPICAL

D & F front

All caution, warning and indicator lights are presented in detail in Figure 1—26.

LEFT

- DRAG CHUTE HANDLE
- AIR REFUELING LIGHTS AND RESET BUTTON
- LANDING GEAR HANDLE
- LANDING GEAR DOWNLOCK OVERRIDE SWITCH
- LANDING & TAXI LIGHT SWITCH
- ANTI SKID SWITCH
- ARRESTING HOOK SWITCH
- JETTISON EXTERNAL STORES BUTTON
- LANDING GEAR POSITION INDICATOR LIGHTS
- GEAR WARNING LIGHT AND BEEPER TEST SWITCH
- EMERGENCY LANDING GEAR EXTENSION HANDLE
- D ONLY added by [948]

RIGHT

- VIDEO PEDESTAL KNOB
- CAUTION LIGHT PANEL
- AC AND DC ELECTRIC POWER CONTROL PANEL
- CAUTION LIGHTS TEST BUTTON

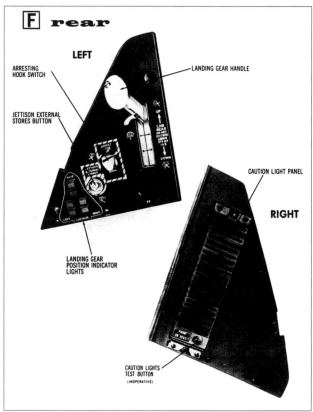

F rear

LEFT

- ARRESTING HOOK SWITCH
- JETTISON EXTERNAL STORES BUTTON
- LANDING GEAR HANDLE
- LANDING GEAR POSITION INDICATOR LIGHTS

RIGHT

- CAUTION LIGHT PANEL
- CAUTION LIGHTS TEST BUTTON (INOPERATIVE)

F-105D/F front auxiliary instrument panels. (USAF)

F-105F rear auxiliary instrument panels. (USAF)

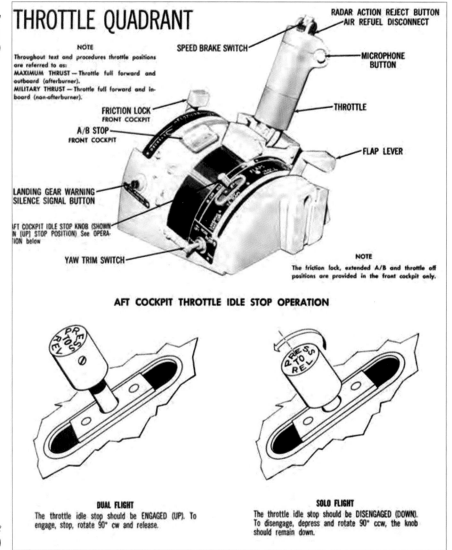

THROTTLE QUADRANT

NOTE
Throughout text and procedures throttle positions are referred to as:
MAXIMUM THRUST — Throttle full forward and outboard (afterburner).
MILITARY THRUST — Throttle full forward and inboard (non-afterburner).

- RADAR ACTION REJECT BUTTON
- AIR REFUEL DISCONNECT
- SPEED BRAKE SWITCH
- MICROPHONE BUTTON
- THROTTLE
- FLAP LEVER
- FRICTION LOCK FRONT COCKPIT
- A/B STOP FRONT COCKPIT
- LANDING GEAR WARNING SILENCE SIGNAL BUTTON
- AFT COCKPIT IDLE STOP KNOB (SHOWN IN [UP] STOP POSITION) See OPERATION below
- YAW TRIM SWITCH

NOTE
The friction lock, extended A/B and throttle off positions are provided in the front cockpit only.

AFT COCKPIT THROTTLE IDLE STOP OPERATION

DUAL FLIGHT
The throttle idle stop should be ENGAGED (UP). To engage, stop, rotate 90° cw and release.

SOLO FLIGHT
The throttle idle stop should be DISENGAGED (DOWN). To disengage, depress and rotate 90° ccw, the knob should remain down.

F-105D/F throttle quadrant. (USAF)

152

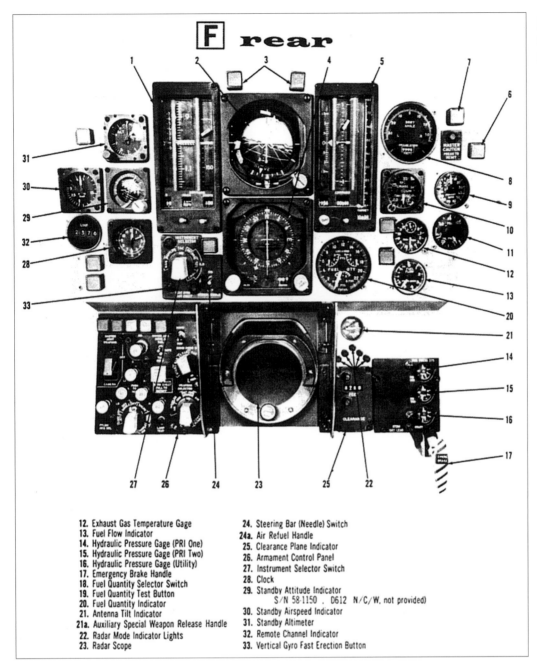

12. Exhaust Gas Temperature Gage
13. Fuel Flow Indicator
14. Hydraulic Pressure Gage (PRI One)
15. Hydraulic Pressure Gage (PRI Two)
16. Hydraulic Pressure Gage (Utility)
17. Emergency Brake Handle
18. Fuel Quantity Selector Switch
19. Fuel Quantity Test Button
20. Fuel Quantity Indicator
21. Antenna Tilt Indicator
21a. Auxiliary Special Weapon Release Handle
22. Radar Mode Indicator Lights
23. Radar Scope

24. Steering Bar (Needle) Switch
24a. Air Refuel Handle
25. Clearance Plane Indicator
26. Armament Control Panel
27. Instrument Selector Switch
28. Clock
29. Standby Attitude Indicator
      S/N 58-1150 . D612 N/C/W, not provided)
30. Standby Airspeed Indicator
31. Standby Altimeter
32. Remote Channel Indicator
33. Vertical Gyro Fast Erection Button

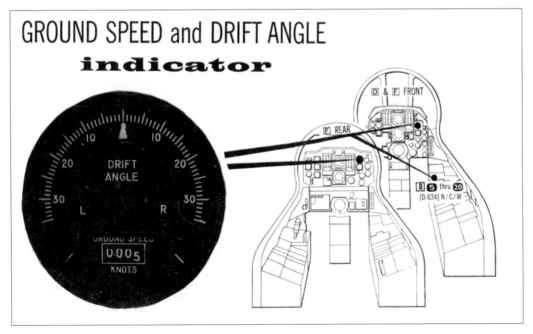

GROUND SPEED and DRIFT ANGLE
indicator

*Ground speed and drift
angle indicator. (USAF)*

153

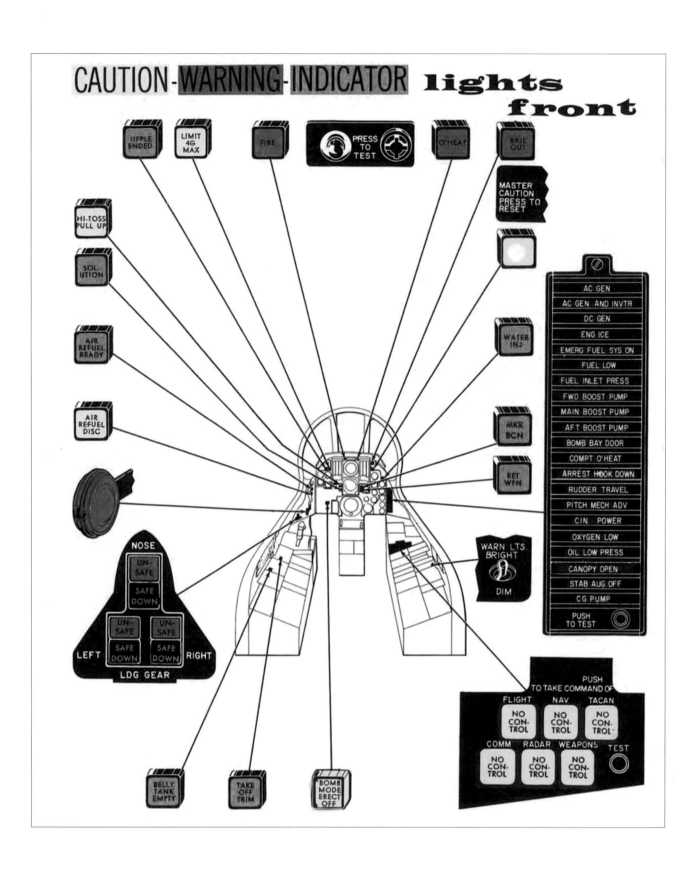

*F-105D/F front caution/
warning indicator lights.
(USAF)*

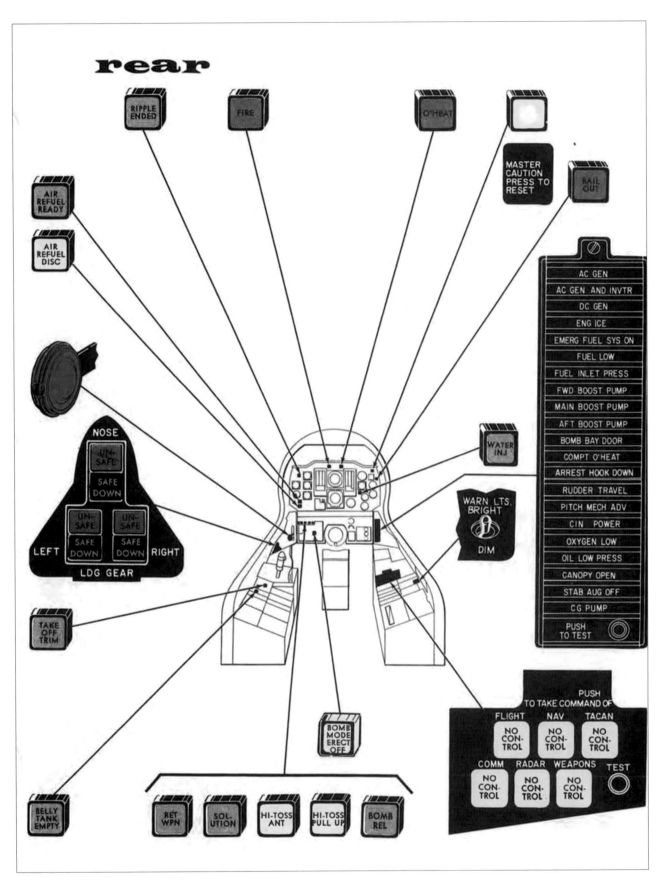

rear

*F-105F rear caution/
warning indicator lights.
(USAF)*

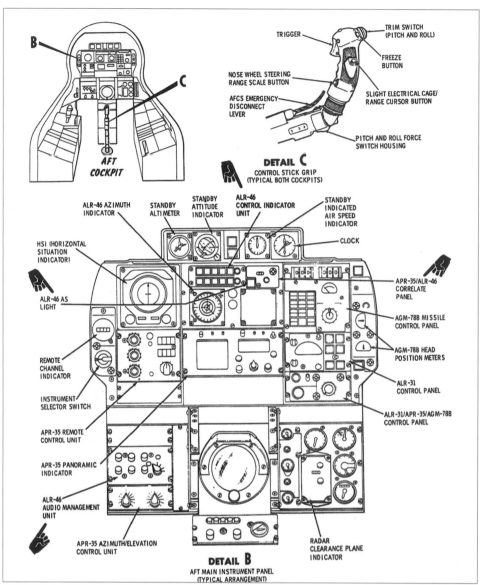

F-105G rear cockpit.
(USAF)

B

C

AFT
COCKPIT

TRIGGER

TRIM SWITCH
(PITCH AND ROLL)

NOSE WHEEL STEERING
RANGE SCALE BUTTON

FREEZE
BUTTON

AFCS EMERGENCY
DISCONNECT
LEVER

SLIGHT ELECTRICAL CAGE/
RANGE CURSOR BUTTON

PITCH AND ROLL FORCE
SWITCH HOUSING

DETAIL C
CONTROL STICK GRIP
(TYPICAL BOTH COCKPITS)

ALR-46 AZIMUTH
INDICATOR

STANDBY
ALTIMETER

STANDBY
ATTITUDE
INDICATOR

ALR-46
CONTROL INDICATOR
UNIT

STANDBY
INDICATED
AIR SPEED
INDICATOR

HSI (HORIZONTAL
SITUATION
INDICATOR)

CLOCK

ALR-46 AS
LIGHT

APR-35/ALR-46
CORRELATE
PANEL

AGM-78B MISSILE
CONTROL PANEL

REMOTE
CHANNEL
INDICATOR

AGM-78B HEAD
POSITION METERS

ALR-31
CONTROL PANEL

INSTRUMENT
SELECTOR SWITCH

ALR-31/APR-35/AGM-78B
CONTROL PANEL

APR-35 REMOTE
CONTROL UNIT

APR-35 PANORAMIC
INDICATOR

ALR-46
AUDIO MANAGEMENT
UNIT

APR-35 AZIMUTH/ELEVATION
CONTROL UNIT

RADAR
CLEARANCE PLANE
INDICATOR

DETAIL B
AFT MAIN INSTRUMENT PANEL
(TYPICAL ARRANGEMENT)

Bottom left:
ARU-2B/A attitude
director indicator.
(USAF)

Bottom right:
Horizontal situation
indicator HSI. (USAF)

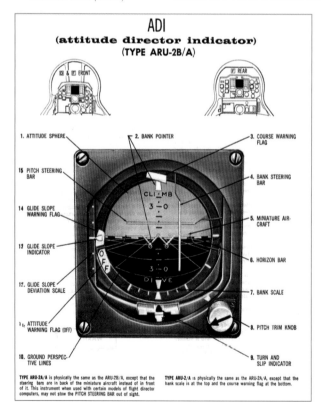

ADI
(attitude director indicator)
(TYPE ARU-2B/A)

D & E FRONT

F REAR

CLIMB
3 · 0

OFF

3 · 0
DIVE

1. ATTITUDE SPHERE
2. BANK POINTER
3. COURSE WARNING FLAG
4. BANK STEERING BAR
5. MINIATURE AIR-CRAFT
6. HORIZON BAR
7. BANK SCALE
8. PITCH TRIM KNOB
9. TURN AND SLIP INDICATOR
10. GROUND PERSPEC-TIVE LINES
11. ATTITUDE WARNING FLAG (OFF)
12. GLIDE SLOPE DEVIATION SCALE
13. GLIDE SLOPE INDICATOR
14. GLIDE SLOPE WARNING FLAG
15. PITCH STEERING BAR

TYPE ARU-2A/A is physically the same as the ARU-2B/A, except that the steering bars are in back of the miniature aircraft instead of in front of it. This instrument when used with certain models of flight director computers, may not stow the PITCH STEERING BAR out of sight.

TYPE ARU-2/A is physically the same as the ARU-2A/A, except that the bank scale is at the top and the course warning flag at the bottom.

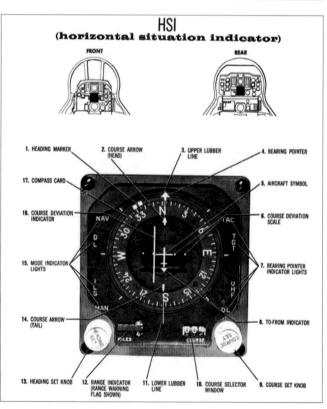

HSI
(horizontal situation indicator)

FRONT

REAR

1. HEADING MARKER
2. COURSE ARROW (HEAD)
3. UPPER LUBBER LINE
4. BEARING POINTER
5. AIRCRAFT SYMBOL
6. COURSE DEVIATION SCALE
7. BEARING POINTER INDICATOR LIGHTS
8. TO-FROM INDICATOR
9. COURSE SET KNOB
10. COURSE SELECTOR WINDOW
11. LOWER LUBBER LINE
12. RANGE INDICATOR (RANGE WARNING FLAG SHOWN)
13. HEADING SET KNOB
14. COURSE ARROW (TAIL)
15. MODE INDICATOR LIGHTS
16. COURSE DEVIATION INDICATOR
17. COMPASS CARD

NAV
DL
ILS
MAN
TAC
TGT
UHF
DL

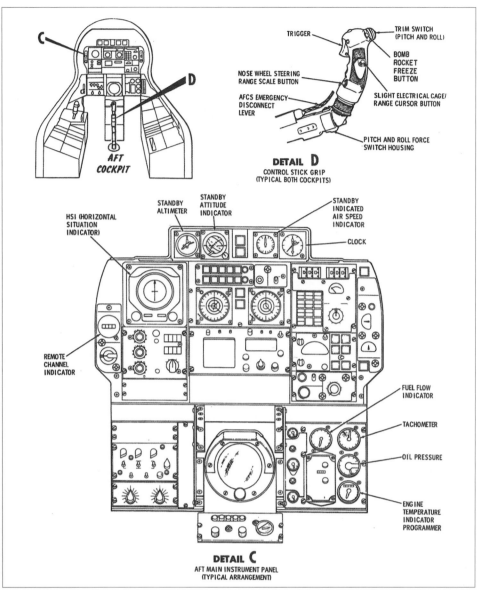

F-105G rear cockpit. (USAF)

TRIGGER

TRIM SWITCH (PITCH AND ROLL)

BOMB ROCKET FREEZE BUTTON

NOSE WHEEL STEERING RANGE SCALE BUTTON

AFCS EMERGENCY DISCONNECT LEVER

SLIGHT ELECTRICAL CAGE/ RANGE CURSOR BUTTON

PITCH AND ROLL FORCE SWITCH HOUSING

AFT COCKPIT

DETAIL D
CONTROL STICK GRIP
(TYPICAL BOTH COCKPITS)

HSI (HORIZONTAL SITUATION INDICATOR)

STANDBY ALTIMETER

STANDBY ATTITUDE INDICATOR

STANDBY INDICATED AIR SPEED INDICATOR

CLOCK

REMOTE CHANNEL INDICATOR

FUEL FLOW INDICATOR

TACHOMETER

OIL PRESSURE

ENGINE TEMPERATURE INDICATOR PROGRAMMER

DETAIL C
AFT MAIN INSTRUMENT PANEL
(TYPICAL ARRANGEMENT)

Bottom left:
Airspeed-Mach indicator AMI. (USAF)

Altitude Vertical Velocity Indicator AVVI. (USAF)

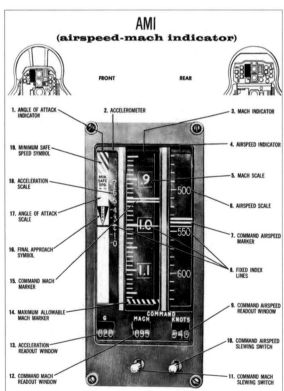

AMI
(airspeed-mach indicator)

FRONT — REAR

1. ANGLE OF ATTACK INDICATOR
2. ACCELEROMETER
3. MACH INDICATOR
19. MINIMUM SAFE SPEED SYMBOL
4. AIRSPEED INDICATOR
18. ACCELERATION SCALE
5. MACH SCALE
17. ANGLE OF ATTACK SCALE
6. AIRSPEED SCALE
16. FINAL APPROACH SYMBOL
7. COMMAND AIRSPEED MARKER
15. COMMAND MACH MARKER
8. FIXED INDEX LINES
14. MAXIMUM ALLOWABLE MACH MARKER
9. COMMAND AIRSPEED READOUT WINDOW
13. ACCELERATION READOUT WINDOW
10. COMMAND AIRSPEED SLEWING SWITCH
12. COMMAND MACH READOUT WINDOW
11. COMMAND MACH SLEWING SWITCH

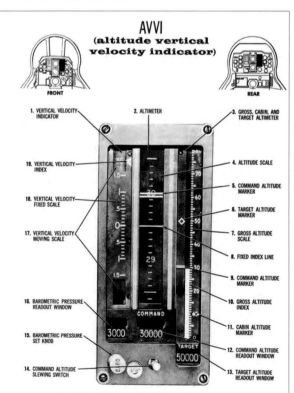

AVVI
(altitude vertical velocity indicator)

FRONT — REAR

1. VERTICAL VELOCITY INDICATOR
2. ALTIMETER
3. GROSS, CABIN, AND TARGET ALTIMETER
19. VERTICAL VELOCITY INDEX
4. ALTITUDE SCALE
18. VERTICAL VELOCITY FIXED SCALE
5. COMMAND ALTITUDE MARKER
17. VERTICAL VELOCITY MOVING SCALE
6. TARGET ALTITUDE MARKER
7. GROSS ALTITUDE SCALE
8. FIXED INDEX LINE
9. COMMAND ALTITUDE MARKER
16. BAROMETRIC PRESSURE READOUT WINDOW
10. GROSS ALTITUDE INDEX
15. BAROMETRIC PRESSURE SET KNOB
11. CABIN ALTITUDE MARKER
12. COMMAND ALTITUDE READOUT WINDOW
14. COMMAND ALTITUDE SLEWING SWITCH
13. TARGET ALTITUDE READOUT WINDOW

157

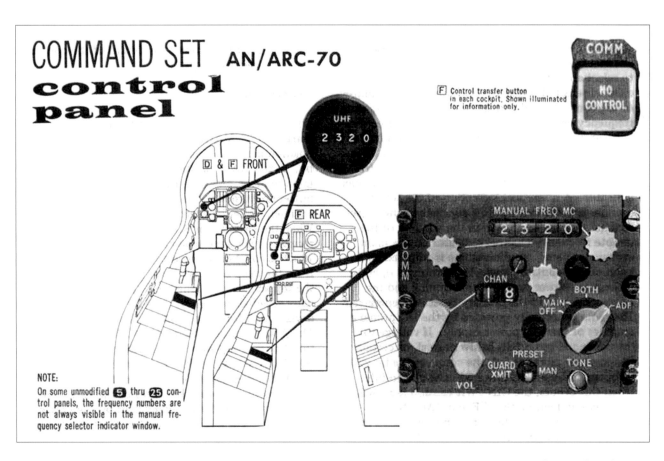

AN/ARC-70 communications radio control panel. (USAF)

AN/APN-131 Doppler navigation system control panel. (USAF)

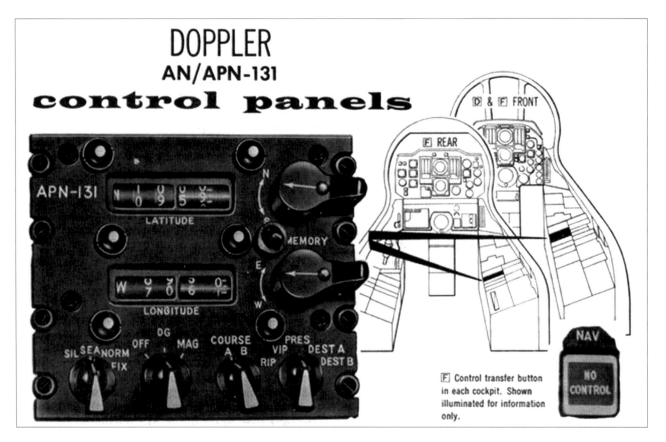

Fire control system

The AN/ASG-19 Thunderstick fire control system was an integration of the R-14A radar system, attack and displays system and toss-bomb computer subsystem. Other aircraft systems provided input for use in or with the fire-control system and the system provided functions for use in other aircraft systems for navigational purposes. The Thunderstick FCS system provided the following all-weather capabilities:

For navigation (using the radar):

- Ground mapping
- Contour mapping
- Terrain avoidance

For bombing (using the Toss-Bomb Computer):

- Visual dive toss (radar or pressure (CADC) ranging)
- Visual identification point (VIP)
- Visual target identification point (VTIP)
- Blind identification point (BIP)
- Blind target identification point (BTIP)
- Manual – used when the fire control system was inoperative
- Timer (timed manual run), used if Toss Bomb Computer was inoperative and/or timed manual retarded weapon delivery.

For air-to-ground attack (visual only)

- Air-to-ground ranging
- Guns-ground
- Rockets-ground
- Missiles-ground

For air-to-air attack:

- This mode consisted of searching, acquiring and tracking a target. The functions were:
- Visual guns – air
- Visual missiles – air
- Blind guns – air
- Blind missiles – air, co-altitude
- Blind missiles – air, snap-up

Compass control panel.
(USAF)

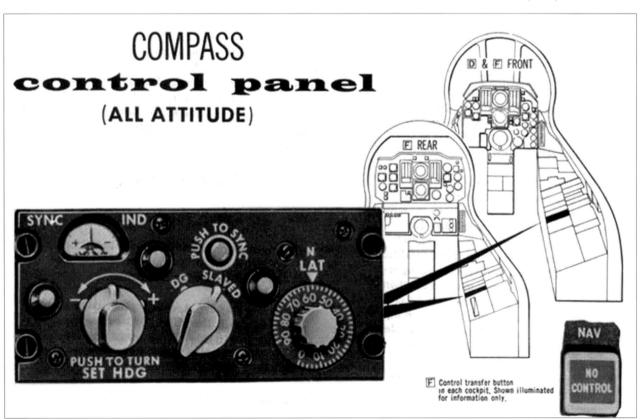

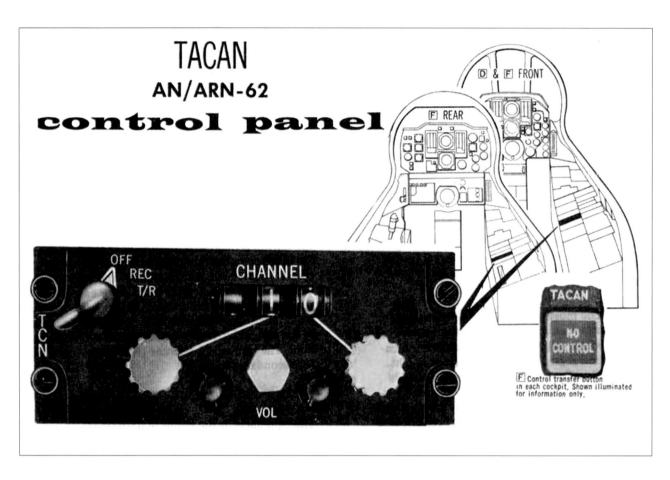

AN/ARN-62 TACAN control panel. (USAF)

AN/APX-37 IFF control panel. (USAF)

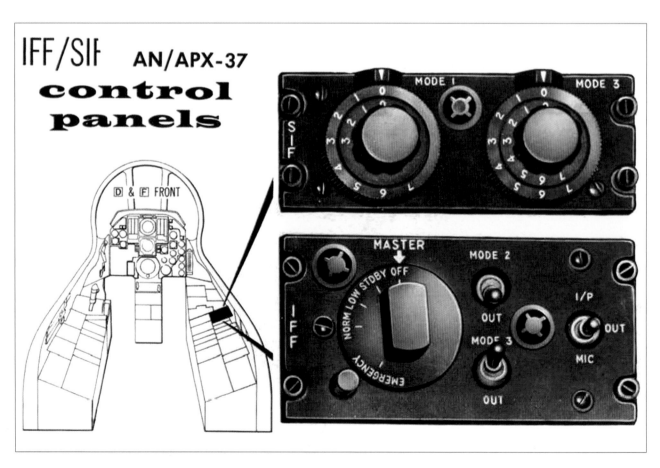

The NASARR R-14A monopulse radiation type X-band radar was an integral part of the fire control system, providing information to the toss-bomb computer and the attack and display subsystems. The navigation modes of the radar – ground mapping, contour mapping and terrain avoidance – provided the pilot with a video display of the terrain below and ahead of the aircraft. In addition to their use for navigation, ground and contour mapping, the radar's navigation modes were used in blind bombing to identify targets and prominent terrain features, and provided range information to the toss-bomb computer. During visual bombing runs the radar provided ranging information to the attack and display subsystems. The search-attack modes were used for air-to-air attacks with gun and missiles, and supplied search, target acquisition and tracking functions in air-to-ground attack with gun, rockets and missiles. The radar provided ranging information to the attack and display subsystem as in the dive bombing mode and information presented on the radar scope was also presented on the sight combining glass, except for ground mapping.

The R-14A radar had two ground map modes – spoil and pencil. The spoil mode presented a 90° sector display of the terrain ahead in scale ranges of 80, 40 or 13 nautical miles. The antenna beam scanned the ground ahead in a pattern 90° in azimuth and 55° in elevation, and was stabilised in roll and pitch. The pilot could vary the antenna beam up 15° and down 30°

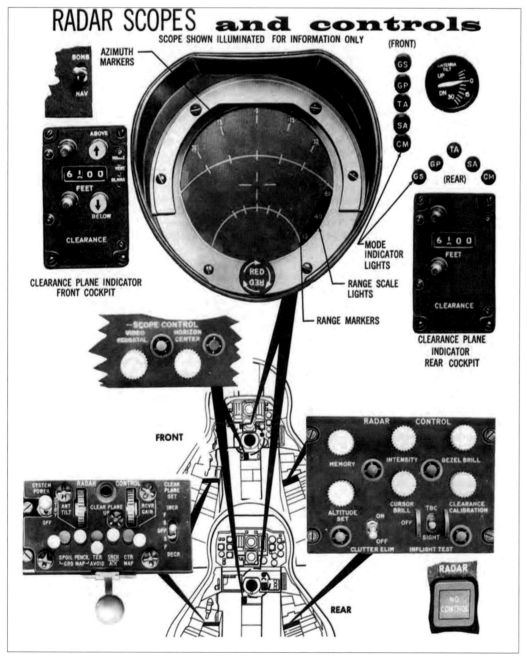

F-105D/F radar scopes and controls. (USAF)

to locate targets. Range and azimuth cursors were displayed on the scope to indicate range, drift angle and offset during bombing attacks.

The pencil mode was the same as the spoil mode, but displayed fewer targets with higher definition, because the antenna vertical spread was reduced from 55 to 6.2°.

The contour map mode presented a 90° sector display of terrain ahead of the aircraft above a selected clearance plane from 0 to 6,000 feet below the aircraft, that was parallel to true horizon thanks to all attitude gyro signals at all times. Only those surfaces that had enough terrain elevation to project into the clearance plane and antenna beam appeared on the radar scope. Range scales of 13 or 40 nautical miles could be selected. This mode was useful for correction of aircraft drift, determination of landmark heights and radar let-downs on airfields surrounded by mountainous terrain. The terrain avoidance mode was similar, but the clearance plane was maintained parallel to the aircraft flight path at all times. This mode enabled the pilot to avoid collision with obstacles such as hills or mountains during low-level flight.

The search/attack mode presented a display of targets in a sector 90° in azimuth and 2.7° above and below the antenna boresight. The effective beam coverage in elevation was 9.4° and the antenna tilt could be controlled from 15° up to 30° down from the armament datum line. This mode functioned as two submodes – search (locating targets) and attack (lock-on to targets). The search could be done blind – using the radar scope (the lock-on was done manually after finding the target) and visual – using the sight combining glass (the lock-on occurred automatically when the target was aligned in the reticle pipper within 8,000-750 yards range).

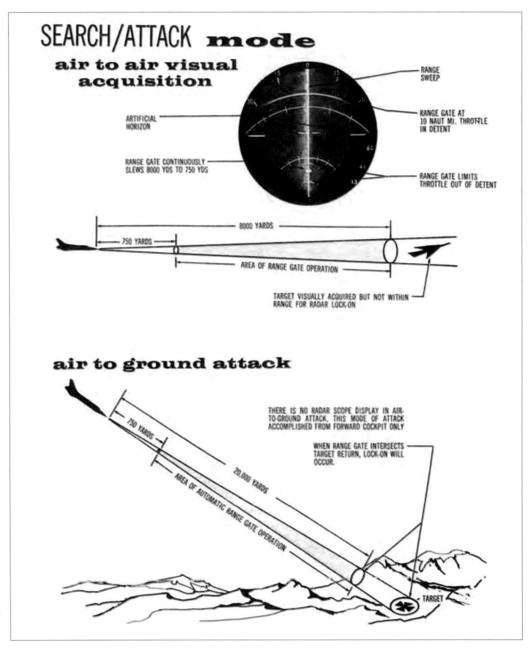

NASARR R-14A radar modes. (USAF)

Technicians maintaining the NASARR R-14A radar. (USAF, Donald Kutyna)

Technicians maintaining the NASARR R-14A radar. (USAF, Donald Kutyna)

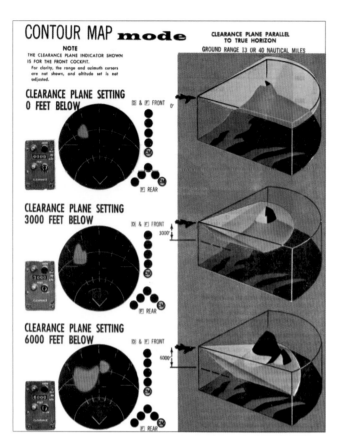

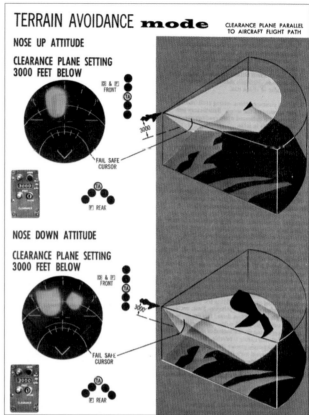

NASARR R-14A radar modes. (USAF)

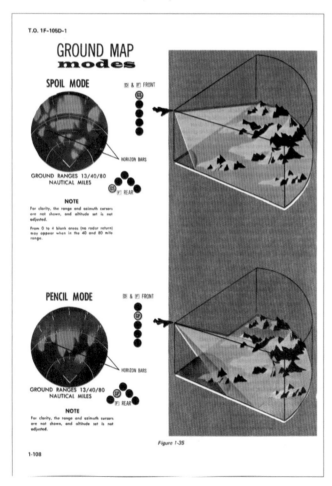

NASARR R-14A radar modes. (USAF)

Technicians maintaining the NASARR R-14A radar. (USAF)

The radar range gate was controlled by twisting the throttle grip clockwise. By twisting it anti-clockwise, the radar was returned from tracking to search. The radar action reject button on the throttle grip was used to acquire or reject a target.

Sight

The sight system added to the fire control system the capability of computing lead pursuit against aerial targets using the cannon and missiles and ground targets (using cannon and rockets). The sight head was also used as an indicator in dive and manual bombing modes and as a secondary indicator in the air-to-air and terrain avoidance modes.

The toss-bomb computer (TBC) provided all-weather store delivery capability for the fire control system. This device automatically computed the aircraft's present position relative to the target and provided a store release signal at the proper time and altitude to provide proper placement of the store on the target. The system operated in five automatic modes, described above.

Armament

The fixed armament comprised one 20 mm General Electric M61A1 Vulcan six-barrel, hydraulically driven rotary cannon, mounted in the forward fuselage. In the F-105D/F, linkless rounds were fed from a large, cylindrical drum, into which spent cases were also returned. The entire drum was winched out of the aircraft for reloading. The rate of fire was 6,000 rpm and the muzzle velocity was 1,030 m/s. The ammunition supply was 1,130 rounds, but usually only 1,028 were loaded, which allowed for 10 seconds of firing.

The F-105 was designed primarily as nuclear strike aircraft, and for this role it could carry one Mk 28IN (later known as B28IN) or Mk 43 (later B43) thermonuclear bomb with yield varying from 70 kilotons to 1.1 megatons in the internal bomb bay and one Mk 57 (later B57) lightweight tactical boosted implosion fission nuclear bomb with yield ranging from 5 to 20 kilotons or Mk 61 (later B61) thermonuclear bomb with yield ranging from 0.3 to 340 kilotons on each inboard wing pylon or the centreline pylon.

F-105D/F fire control and associated systems scheme. (USAF)

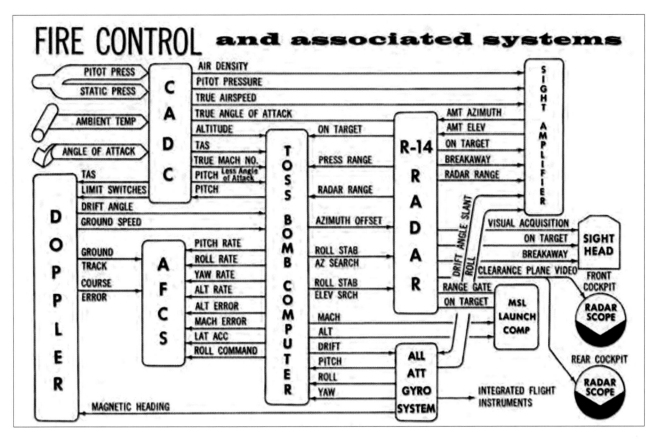

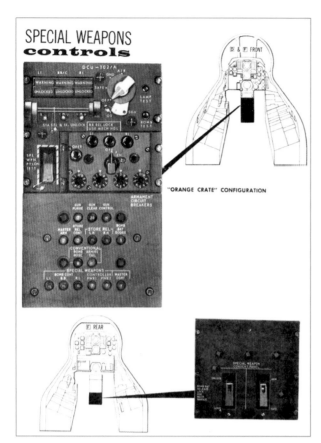

F-105D/F special weapons controls. (USAF)

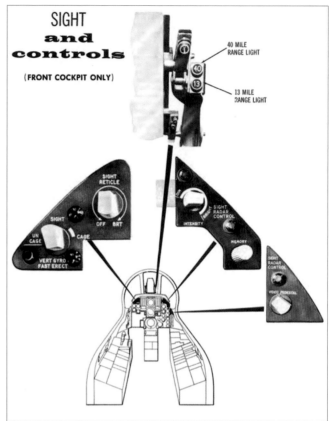

F-105D/F sight and its controls. (USAF)

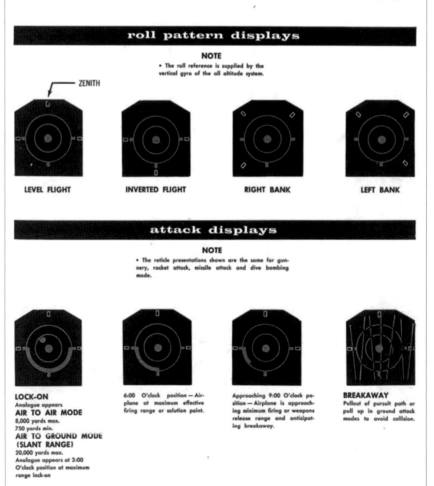

F-105D/F sight reticle displays. (USAF)

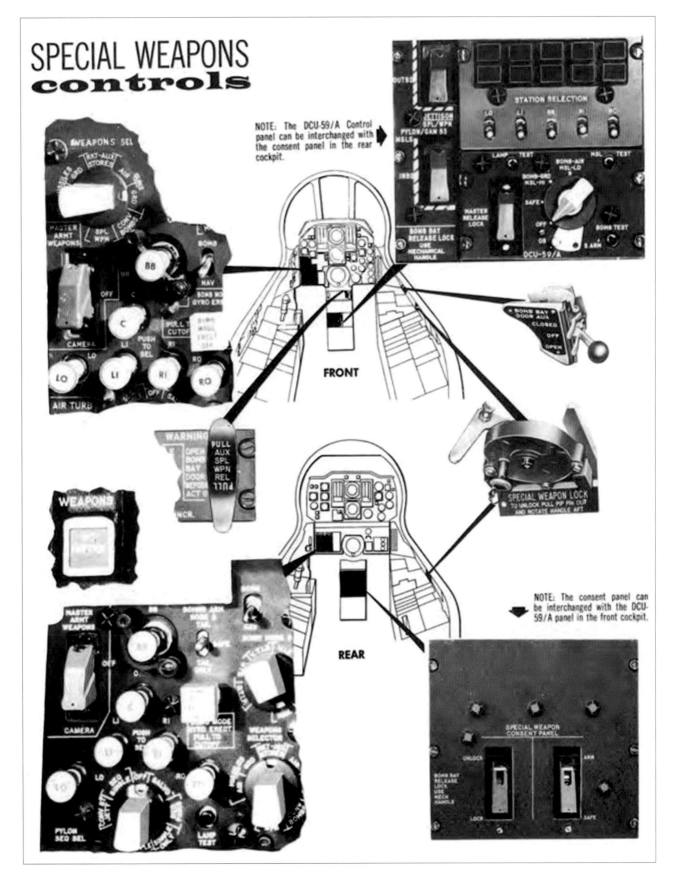

SPECIAL WEAPONS
controls

NOTE: The DCU-59/A Control panel can be interchanged with the consent panel in the rear cockpit.

FRONT

NOTE: The consent panel can be interchanged with the DCU-59/A panel in the front cockpit.

REAR

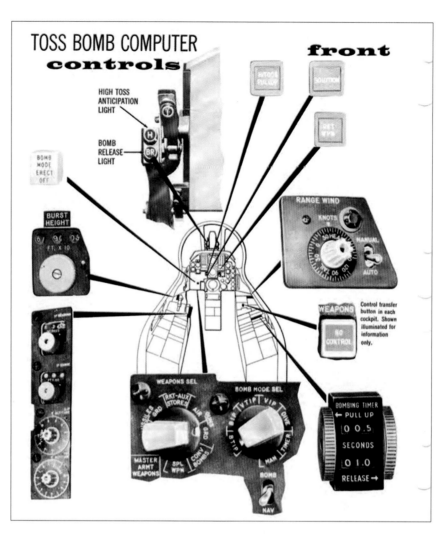

F-105D/F toss-bomb controls. (USAF)

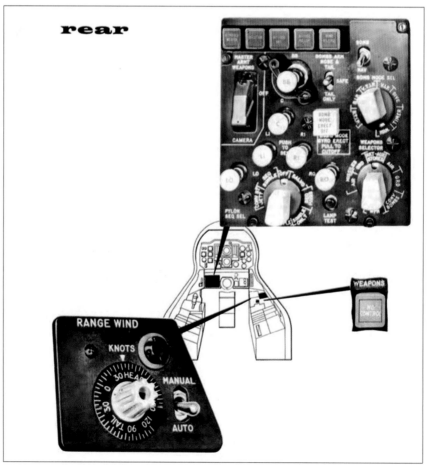

ARMAMENT controls

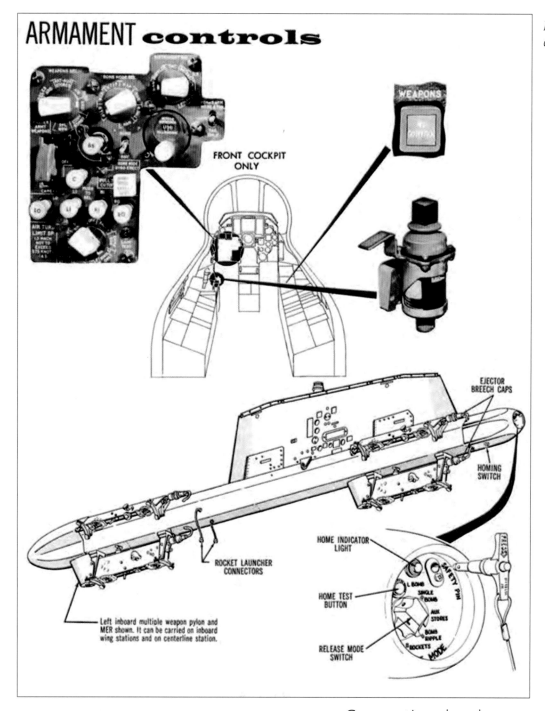

FRONT COCKPIT ONLY

EJECTOR BREECH CAPS

HOMING SWITCH

HOME INDICATOR LIGHT

ROCKET LAUNCHER CONNECTORS

HOME TEST BUTTON

Left inboard multiple weapon pylon and MER shown. It can be carried on inboard wing stations and on centerline station.

RELEASE MODE SWITCH

Conventional ordnance

Apart from nuclear weapons, the F-105 could carry all types of conventional munitions of that time – M117 750 lb (340 kg), M118 3,000 lb (1,360 kg) general purpose bombs, Mk 81 250 lb (113 kg), Mk 82 500 lb (227 kg), Mk 83 1,000 lb (454 kg), Mk 84 2,000 lb (907 kg) low-drag general purpose bombs, Mk 82SE 570lb 'Snakeye' general purpose high-drag bombs, cluster bomb dispensers – SUU-30A with CBU-24 munitions or SUU-30HB with CBU-71 munitions, SUU-21 practice bomb dispenser – BLU-31 mines, BLU-1/B and BLU-27 napalm bombs, MC-1 and BLU-52 chemical bombs, M129 leaflet bombs LAU-32 or LAU-52 seven-tube and LAU-3/A or LAU-18/A 19-tube unguided rocket launchers, AGM-12 B/C Bullpup guided air-to-ground missiles on pylon adapters, AIM-9B/E Sidewinder heat-seeking air-to-air missiles. AGM-45A Shrike and AGM-78 Standard ARM anti-radiation missiles with on-pylon adapters could be carried by Wild Weasel variants. The ordnance was carried on five stations – the centreline and two underwing pylons. On the centreline and inboard pylons, Multiple Ejector Racks (MER) could be mounted to increase the bomb, mine or rocket carrying ability on those stations.

Types of ordnance carried on respective stations:

Centreline pylon – a multiple ejection rack (MER) with either:
- 6x M117 bombs, or 6x Mk 82 or Mk 82 'Snakeye' bombs
- 3x Mk 83 bombs or one Mk 84 bomb or one M118 bomb
- 6x M129 leaflet bombs, MC-1 chemical bombs or MLU-32 flares
- 5x SUU-30 with CBU-24, – 29, – 49, – 53 or – 64 cluster bomblets
- 3x BLU-1/B or 2x BLU-27 napalm bombs, or 3x BLU-31 mines
- One SUU-21 practice bomb dispenser

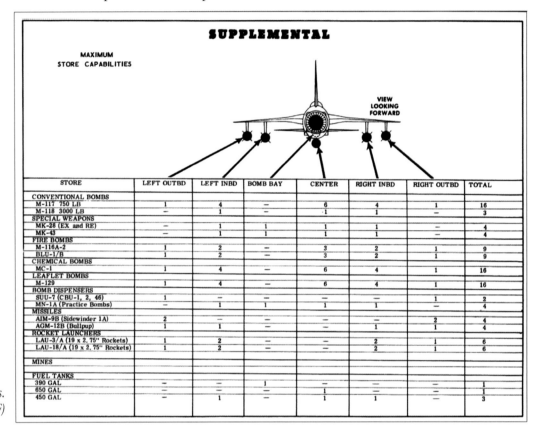

SUPPLEMENTAL

MAXIMUM STORE CAPABILITIES

VIEW LOOKING FORWARD

STORE	LEFT OUTBD	LEFT INBD	BOMB BAY	CENTER	RIGHT INBD	RIGHT OUTBD	TOTAL
CONVENTIONAL BOMBS							
M-117 750 LB	1	4	–	6	4	1	16
M-118 3000 LB	–	1	–	1	1	–	3
SPECIAL WEAPONS							
MK-28 (EX and RE)	–	1	1	1	1	–	4
MK-43	–	1	1	1	1	–	4
FIRE BOMBS							
M-116A-2	1	2	–	3	2	1	9
BLU-1/B	1	2	–	3	2	1	9
CHEMICAL BOMBS							
MC-1	1	4	–	6	4	1	16
LEAFLET BOMBS							
M-129	1	4	–	6	4	1	16
BOMB DISPENSERS							
SUU-7 (CBU-1, 2, 46)	1	–	–	–	–	1	2
MN-1A (Practice Bombs)	–	1	1	1	1	–	4
MISSILES							
AIM-9B (Sidewinder 1A)	2	–	–	–	–	2	4
AGM-12B (Bullpup)	1	1	–	–	1	1	4
ROCKET LAUNCHERS							
LAU-3/A (19 x 2.75" Rockets)	1	2	–	–	2	1	6
LAU-18/A (19 x 2.75" Rockets)	1	2	–	–	2	1	6
MINES							
FUEL TANKS							
390 GAL	–	–	1	–	–	–	1
650 GAL	–	–	–	1	–	–	1
450 GAL	–	1	–	1	1	–	3

F-105D/F loadouts. (USAF)

SUPPLEMENTAL

MAXIMUM STORE CAPABILITIES

VIEW LOOKING FORWARD

STORE	LEFT OUTBD	LEFT INBD	BOMB BAY	CENTER	RIGHT INBD	RIGHT OUTBD	TOTAL
SPECIAL WEAPONS							
MK-61	–	1	–	1	1	–	3
MK-57	–	–	–	1	–	–	1
CONVENTIONAL BOMBS							
MK 82 L.D.	1	4	–	6	4	1	16
MK 82 SNAKEYE M.D.	1	4	–	6	4	1	16
MK 83	1	2	–	3	2	1	9
MK 84	–	1	–	1	1	–	3
M-117 RETARDED	1	–	–	3	–	1	5
M-117 DESTRUCTOR	1	–	–	3	–	1	5
FIRE BOMBS							
BLU-27 (Finned & Unfinned)	1	2	–	2	2	1	8
CHEMICAL BOMBS							
BLU-52	1	2	–	2	2	1	8
A/B 45Y-2 (Spray Tank)	1	–	–	–	–	1	2
BOMB DISPENSERS							
SUU-10 (CBU-3)	1	–	–	–	–	1	2
SUU-30 (CBU 24, 29, 49, 53, 54)	1	4	–	5	4	1	15
SUU-13 (CBU-3, 7, 28, 37)	1	–	–	–	–	1	2
SUU-21 (Training)	1	1	–	1	1	1	5
MISSILES							
AIM-9E	2	–	–	–	–	2	4
AGM-12C	–	1	–	–	1	–	2
AGM-45A	–	–	–	–	–	1	2

- One 450-gal or 650-gal fuel tank

Inboard wing pylons– each could carry either:

- 4x Mk 82/Mk 82 'Snakeye' or M117 on a MER, or 2x Mk 83 or one Mk 84 bomb.
- One M118 bomb
- 4x SUU-30 CBU dispensers (CBU-24, 29, 49, 53, 54)
- 2x BLU-27 or BLU-1/B napalm bombs, 2x BLU-52 or 4x MC – chemical bombs, M129 dispensers or BLU-31 mines
- 2x LAU-32, LAU-52, LAU-3/A or LAU-18/A unguided rocket launchers

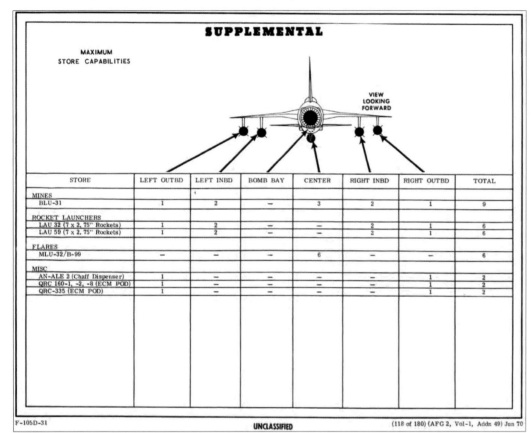

F-105D/F loadouts. (USAF)

F-105D (58-1173) during weapon trials with a maximum load of sixteen 750-lb M117 bombs. Such a loadout was never used in actual combat due to excessive drag produced by the bombs and lack of external fuel tanks. (USAF)

- 1x AGM-12B/C Bullpup air-to-ground missile (with pylon adapter)
- The F-105 F/G could also carry the AGM-78 Standard ARM anti-radiation missile on a pylon adapter.

Outboard wing pylons – each could carry either:
- 1x Mk 82, Mk 83 or M117 bomb
- 1x BLU-27 or BLU-1/B fire bomb
- 1x BLU-52 chemical bomb or 1x SUU-10 (CBU-3) or SUU-30 (CBU-24,-29, – 49, – 53, – 54) dispenser or M129 leaflet bomb
- 1x AIM-9B or AIM-9E Sidewinder air-to-air missile (or two on a dual launcher)
- 1x LAU-3 2.75in rocket launcher
- 1x AGM-12B/C Bullpup air-to-ground missile or AGM-45A Shrike anti-radiation missile

During the Vietnam war the most typical loadouts were:
- Centreline MER with 6xM117 or Mk 82 or 3xMk 83 bombs
- Two 450-gal drop tanks on inboard underwing pylons

Armourers load practice Mk 82 bombs on a F-105G from the 128th TFS, Georgia ANG in 1982. (DoD)

- 2x Mk 82, Mk 83 or M117 bomb on outboard pylons
- Two M118 bombs on inboard underwing pylons and one 650-gal tank on centreline pylon (this was used mainly against hardened targets)
- Centreline MER with 6x SUU-30 dispensers with CBU-24 munitions
- Two 450-gal drop tanks on inboard underwing pylons
- ALQ-71 ECM pod on outboard pylon (this was used on Wild Weasel missions against enemy SAM batteries)
- Two 450-gal drop tanks on inboard underwing pylons
- Two AGM-45A Shrike anti-radiation missiles on outboard pylons (this was used on Wild Weasel missions against enemy radars)
- Two AGM-78 Standard ARM anti-radiation missiles on inboard pylons
- Two AGM-45A Shrike anti-radiation missiles on outboard pylons
- One 650-gal centreline tank
- (This was used on Wild Weasel missions against enemy radars)

Armourers load practice Mk 82 bombs on an F-105G from the 128th TFS, Georgia ANG in 1982. (DoD)

An F-105D with associated weapons and maintenance vehicles. (USAF)

Republic F-105F (62-4422) with armament layout in August 1964. Armament includes 20mm cannon rounds, 2.75in rockets, AGM-12 Bullpup and AIM-9 Sidewinder missiles, general purpose bomb, cluster bombs, LAU-3A rocket launchers, flare and chaff dispensers and drop tanks. (USAF)

*Bombs and rockets
carried by the F-105D.
(USAF)*

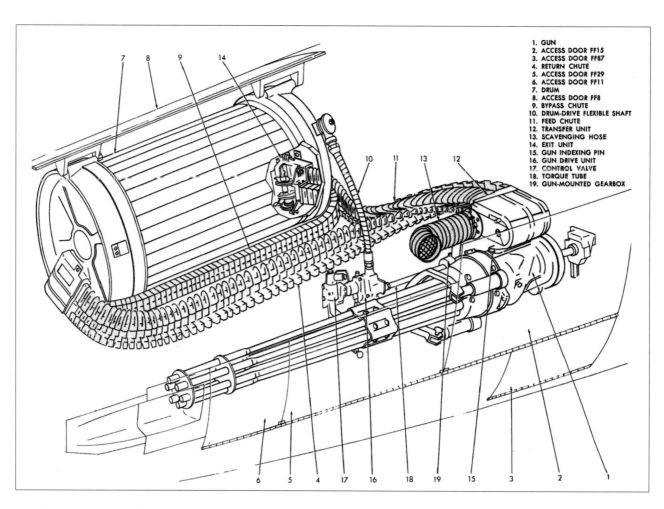

1. GUN
2. ACCESS DOOR FF15
3. ACCESS DOOR FF87
4. RETURN CHUTE
5. ACCESS DOOR FF29
6. ACCESS DOOR FF11
7. DRUM
8. ACCESS DOOR FF8
9. BYPASS CHUTE
10. DRUM-DRIVE FLEXIBLE SHAFT
11. FEED CHUTE
12. TRANSFER UNIT
13. SCAVENGING HOSE
14. EXIT UNIT
15. GUN INDEXING PIN
16. GUN DRIVE UNIT
17. CONTROL VALVE
18. TORQUE TUBE
19. GUN-MOUNTED GEARBOX

Top: F-105D/F *cannon installation. (USAF)*

Bottom: F-105B *cannon installation. (USAF)*

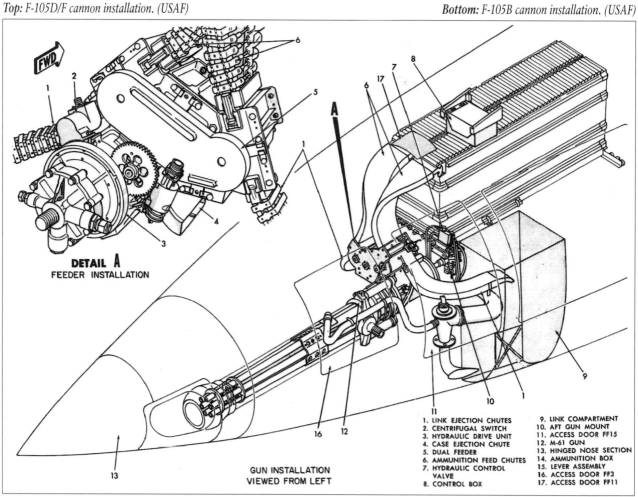

FWD.

DETAIL A
FEEDER INSTALLATION

GUN INSTALLATION
VIEWED FROM LEFT

1. LINK EJECTION CHUTES
2. CENTRIFUGAL SWITCH
3. HYDRAULIC DRIVE UNIT
4. CASE EJECTION CHUTE
5. DUAL FEEDER
6. AMMUNITION FEED CHUTES
7. HYDRAULIC CONTROL VALVE
8. CONTROL BOX

9. LINK COMPARTMENT
10. AFT GUN MOUNT
11. ACCESS DOOR FF15
12. M-61 GUN
13. HINGED NOSE SECTION
14. AMMUNITION BOX
15. LEVER ASSEMBLY
16. ACCESS DOOR FF3
17. ACCESS DOOR FF11

Six 750-lb M117 bombs on the centreline MER. Two are fitted with fuse extenders for detonation above the ground. (Donald Kutyna archive via MLP)

QRC-160 jamming pod. (USAF Museum)

F-105D-15-RE (61-0095) with full load of Mk 82 bombs during weapon trials. (USAF)

AIM-9B Sidewinder heat-seeking air-to-air missiles on a double rail launcher on the starboard outer underwing pylon. (USAF)

Chapter 8 –
F-105 paint schemes
and markings

After the introduction into service in the 1950s and 1960s, F-105s, like all US Air Force jets, were maintained in natural metal finish with large USAF insignia and colourful unit markings. Under Project Look Alike the aircraft were painted in silver lacquer (FS 17178) to prevent corrosion and moisture seepage. Until 1965, so-called 'buzz numbers' consisting of the letters FH (code assigned to the F-105) and three-digit number (e.g. FH-217) were painted in black (FS 37038) on the nose. The upper side of the fuselage was painted olive drab (FS 34087). Some squadrons applied non-regulation markings, such as shark-mouth designs.

In 1965, when the Thuds were involved in the Vietnam conflict on a large scale, South-East Asia (SEA) camouflage was applied to them. This camouflage consisted of large patches of Tan (FS 30219), Dark Green (FS 34079), and Medium Green (FS 34102) on the upper surfaces, and Camouflage Gray (FS 36622) underneath. Some wore 'reversed pattern' camouflage, with green and brown colours in changed positions. The national insignia were reduced in size to 15in diameter and only small black 'USAF' and serial numbers were painted on the vertical fin. No unit markings were applied. In 1967 Ryan's Raiders' aircraft, operating at night, had green and tan patterns applied on the undersides. In 1967 the USAF adopted tail codes – two letters, denoting a squadron, painted in 24in white or light grey block letters on the fin. Below the code letters was the serial number in 15in white letters. Squadrons based at Korat had tail codes beginning with J and squadrons based at Takhli with R (see Appendix 3). On some aircraft individual names and nose art were painted on the forward fuselage sides, upper forward fuselage and air intakes. In 1972 all tactical USAF aircraft operating from Korat RTAFB, including the F-105G Wild Weasels, had 'sharkmouths' painted on the nose. The markings were used until the end of the type's service life, although after the war the colour was changed to black.

After the war some of the F-105s received new camouflage, reflecting possible future operations. European One comprised Europe One Gray (FS 36081), Medium Green (FS 34102) and Gunship Green (FS 34092). The national insignia were applied in all-black low visibility versions. Others remained in SEA camouflage. Unit markings were minimal, usually in the form of a coloured band around the nose or upper fin. Some aircraft retained the wartime nose art, but on others they were removed or changed e.g. the F-105D-6-RE (59-1822) 'The Polish Glider', flown by Maj. Donald Kutyna from the 44th TFS, 355th TFW at Takhli in 1970, was later renamed 'Superhog' when flying with Virginia ANG).

FS 17178

FS 37038

FS 34087

FS 30219

FS 34079

FS 34102

FS 36622

FS 36081

FS 34092

F-105D-10RE (60-0505) in early version of SEA camouflage. (USAF)

YF-105A

Wingspan	34 ft 11 in (10.64 m)
Length	61 ft 5 in (18.72 m)
Wing area	385 ft² (35.76 m²)
Height	19 ft 8 in (5.33 m)
Empty weight	21,010 lb (9,530 kg)
Combat weight (basic mission)	28,966 lb (13,139 kg)
Maximum take-off weight	41,500 lb (18,824 kg)
Service ceiling	49,950 ft (15,220 m)
Maximum speed	778 kt (1,440 km/h) at sea level, 857 kt (1,587 km/h) at 36,000 ft (11,800 m)
Fuel	Internal: 4,391 l (1,160 US gal), Bomb bay tank: 1,476 l (390 US gal), External tanks: 1,550 US gal (5,867 l) – two 450 US gal (1,703 l) underwing tanks, one 650 US gal (2,460 l) centreline tank, Maximum: 11,735 l (3,100 US gal)
Combat radius with external tanks	646 NM (1,204 km)
Ferry range	1,935 NM (3,583 km) with 2,900 US gal of fuel
Powerplant	Pratt& Whitney J57-P-25, rated at 66.kN 15,000 lb (15,000 lb)

	F-105B	F-105D	F-105F	F-105G
Wingspan	34 ft 11 in (10.64 m)	34 ft 11 in (10.64 m)	34 ft 11 in (10.64 m)	34 ft 11 in (10.64 m)
Length	63 ft 1 in (19.22 m)	63 ft 1 in (19.22 m)	69 ft 4 in (21.13 m)	69 ft 4 in (21.13 m)
Wing area	385 ft² (35.76 m²)	385 ft² (35.76 m²)	385 ft² (35.76 m²)	385 ft² (35.76 m²)
Height	19 ft 8 in (5.99 m)	19 ft 8 in (5.99 m)	20 ft 1 in (6.12 m)	20 ft 1 in (6.12 m)
Empty weight	25,855 lb (11,635 kg)	26,855 lb (12,181 kg)	30,419 lb (13,798 kg)	31,279 lb (14,188 kg)
Combat weight (basic mission)	34,870 lb (15,817 kg)	35,637 lb (16,165 kg)		
Maximum take-off weight	52,000 lb (23,400 kg)	52,838 lb (23,967 kg)	45,100 ft (13,746 m)	54,580 lb (24,757 kg)
Service ceiling	48,100 ft (14,670 m)	48,500 ft (14,783 m)	13,746 m (45,100 ft)	43,900 ft (13,380 m)
Maximum speed	In clean configuration 750 kt (1, kt (2,213 km/h) at 36,000 ft (11,800 m)389 km/h) at sea level, 1,195 Maximum combat speed 750 kt (1,389 km/h)	In clean configuration: 726 kt (1,344 km/h) at sea level, 1,199 kt (2,220 km/h) at 36,000 ft (11,800 m), Maximum combat speed 726 kt (1,344 km/h)	In clean configuration: 681 kt (1,261km/h) at sea level, 1,192 kt (2,207 km/h) at 36,000 ft (11,800 m), Maximum combat speed 1,261 km/h (681 kt)	In clean configuration: 681 kt (1,261km/h) at sea level, 1,192 kt (2,207 km/h) at 36,000 ft (11,800 m), Maximum combat speed 681 kt (1,261 km/h)
Fuel	Internal: 1,160 US gal (4,391 l) Bomb bay tank: 390 US gal (1,476 l) External tanks: 1,550 US gal (5,867 l) – two 450 US gal (1,703 l) underwing tanks, one 650 US gal (2,460 l) centreline tank Maximum: 3,100 US gal (11,735 l)	Internal: 1,160 US gal (4,391 l) Bomb bay tank: 390 US gal (1,476 l) External tanks: 1,550 US gal (5,867 l) – two 450 US gal (1,703 l) underwing tanks, one 650 US gal (2,460 l) centreline tank Maximum: 3,100 US gal (11,735 l)	Internal: 1,160 US gal (4,391 l) Bomb bay tank: 390 US gal (1,476 l) External tanks: 1,550 US gal (5,867 l) – two 450 US gal (1,703 l) underwing tanks, one 650 US gal (2,460 l) centreline tank Maximum: 3,100 US gal (11,735 l)	Internal: 1,051 US gal (3,978 l) Bomb bay: 375 US gal (1,419 l) External tanks: 1,550 US gal (5,867 l) – two 450 US gal (1,703 l) underwing tanks, one 650 US gal (2,460 l) centreline tank Maximum: 2,976 US gal (11,265 l)
Combat radius with external tanks	646 NM (1,204 km)	1,252 km (676 NM)	459 NM (850 km)	459 NM (850 km)
Ferry range	1,935 NM (3,583 km) with 2,900 US gal of fuel	1,917 NM (3,550 km) with 3,100 US gal of fuel	1,623 NM (3,005 km) with 3,100 US gal of fuel	1,300 NM (2,408 km) with 2,976 US gal of fuel
Powerplant	Pratt & Whitney J75-P-19 turbojet rated at 16,100 lb (71.6 kN) dry thrust and 24,500 lb (109 kN) with afterburner	Pratt&Whitney J75 – P-19W turbojet rated at 16,100 lb (71.6 kN) dry thrust, 24,500 lb (109 kN) with afterburner and 26,500 lb (118 kN) with afterburner and water injection on take-off	Pratt&Whitney J75 – P-19W turbojet rated at 16,100 lb (71.6 kN) dry thrust, 24,500 lb (109 kN) with afterburner and 26,500 lb (118 kN) with afterburner and water injection on take-off	Pratt&Whitney J75 – P-19W turbojet rated at 16,100 lb (71.6 kN) dry thrust, 24,500 lb (109 kN) with afterburner and 26,500 lb (118 kN) with afterburner and water injection on take-off
Armament	20 mm M61 Vulcan cannon with 1,075 rounds, one 3,400 lb (1,542 kg) Mk28IN (B28IN) or B43 nuclear bomb in the internal bomb bay or up to 12,000 lb (5,442 kg) of ordnance on one centreline and four underwing pylons.	20 mm M61 Vulcan cannon with 1,028 rounds, one 1,542 kg (3,400 lb) Mk28IN or B43 nuclear bomb in the internal bomb bay or up to 12,000 lb (5,442 kg) of ordnance on one centreline and four underwing pylons.	20 mm M61 Vulcan cannon with 1,028 rounds, one 3,400 lb (1,542 kg) Mk28IN or nuclear bomb in the internal bomb bay or up to 12,000 lb (5,442 kg) of ordnance on one centreline and four underwing pylons	20 mm M61 Vulcan cannon with 1,075 rounds, one 3,400 lb (1,542 kg) Mk28IN nuclear bomb in the internal bomb bay or up to 12,000 lb (5,442 kg) of ordnance on one centreline and four underwing pylons.

Appendix 1 – F-105B units

F-105D-5REs from 335th TFS "Chiefs" in natural metal finish – the original F-105 livery. (USAF)

US Air Force:
- 4th Tactical Fighter Wing, Seymour Johnson AFB
- 333rd Tactical Fighter Squadron (1959–1964)
- 334th Tactical Fighter Squadron (1959–1964)
- 335th Tactical Fighter Squadron (1958–1961)
- 336th Tactical Fighter Squadron (1959–1964)
- 4520th Air Demonstration Squadron 'Thunderbirds' Nellis AFB 1963–1964

US Air Force Reserve:
- 508th Tactical Fighter Wing/419th Tactical Fighter Wing, Hill AFB
- 466th Tactical Fighter Squadron (1973–1981).

Air National Guard:
- 108th Tactical Fighter Group, New Jersey ANG, McGuire AFB
- 141st Tactical Fighter Squadron 1964–1981
- 177th Tactical Fighter Group, New Jersey ANG, Atlantic City International Airport
- 119st Tactical Fighter Squadron 1970–1973

Appendix 2 – F-105D/F/G units

US Air Force

4th Tactical Fighter Wing, Seymour Johnson AFB
- 333rd Tactical Fighter Squadron (Jan 1961–Dec 1965 – reassigned permanently to 355th TFW, Takhli RTAFB)
- 334th Tactical Fighter Squadron (Jan 1964–Nov 1966) temporarily deployed (TDY) to Takhli RTAFB August 1965–Feb 1966.
- 335th Tactical Fighter Squadron (June 1960–Nov 1966) TDY to Takhli RTAFB Nov-Dec 1965.
- 336th Tactical Fighter Squadron (Jan 1964–Nov 1966)

8th Tactical Fighter Wing, Itazuke AB, Japan
- 35th Tactical Fighter Squadron
- 36th Tactical Fighter Squadron (Jan 1963–June 1964, to Takhli RTAFB May 1964–June 1964)
- 80th Tactical Fighter Squadron (Jan 1964–Feb 1964) Transferred to Yokota AB in February 1964 without any wing assignment, then to Korat RTAFB in Thailand in May 1964 to June 1964. Returned to Yokota, where it remained until December 1967.

- 18th Tactical Fighter Wing, Kadena AB, Okinawa
- 12th Tactical Fighter Squadron (Oct 1962–1973). TDY to Da Nang 25 December 1964 as Det2, 18th TFW. TDY to Korat, via Da Nang, 1 February to 15 March and 15 June to 25 August 1965. Augmented Korat *Wild Weasel* operations in 1970.
- 44th Tactical Fighter Squadron (1963–1970). First F-105s TDY to Thailand 20–30 April 1964. TDY to Da Nang (as Det 2, 18th TFW) and Korat 18 December 1964–25 February 1965. TDY to 6234th TFW Korat, 21 April–23 June and 10–29 December 1965.

23rd Tactical Fighter Wing, McConnell AFB
- 561st Tactical Fighter Squadron TDY to Korat RTAFB March 1965–July 1965.
- 562nd Tactical Fighter Squadron (Feb 1964–July 1972). TDY to Takhli RTAFB Aug 1965–Dec 1965
- 563rd Tactical Fighter Squadron (Feb 1964–July 1972). TDY to Takhli RTAFB March 1965–Aug 1965

36th Tactical Fighter Wing, Bitburg AB, Germany (May 1961–Dec 1966)
- 22nd Tactical Fighter Squadron
- 23rd Tactical Fighter Squadron
- 53rd Tactical Fighter Squadron

49th Tactical Fighter Wing, Spangdahlem AB, Germany (Oct 1961–Sept 1967)
- 7th Tactical Fighter Squadron
- 8th Tactical Fighter Squadron
- 9th Tactical Fighter Squadron

57th Fighter Weapons Wing, Nellis AFB, Nevada (Feb 1966–Oct 1971)
- 4537th Fighter Weapons Squadron (the Willie Weasel College)

41st Air Division/6441st Tactical Fighter Wing, Yokota AB, Japan
- 35th Tactical Fighter Squadron – TDY to Korat 24 September to 29 November 1964. TDY to Takhli (6235th TFW) 4 May to 26 June 1965 and 19 October to 15 November 1965.
- 36th Tactical Fighter Squadron – TDY to Korat 12 August to 5 October. TDY to Takhli 6 March to 4 May 1965 and 17 August to 28 October 1965.
- 80th Tactical Fighter Squadron – TDY to Korat 30 October to 29 December 1964. TDY to Takhli 27 June to 26 August 1965.

355th Tactical Fighter Wing, Takhli RTAFB, Thailand (replaced 6235th TFW, which managed Takhli temporary deployments from 8 April to 8 November 1965)
- 333rd Tactical Fighter Squadron (Dec 1965–Dec 1970)
- 357th Tactical Fighter Squadron (Jan 1966–Dec 1970)
- 354th Tactical Fighter Squadron (March 1965–Dec 1970) TDY to Kadena 3 March 1965, with rotations to Korat. Redeployed to Korat by April 1965 (6234th TFW). Relocated permanently to Takhli 27 November 1965 – 14 December 1970.
- 44th Tactical Fighter Squadron (Oct 1969–Dec 1970 – transferred from 388th TFS)

388th Tactical Fighter Wing, Korat RTAFB, Thailand (replaced 6234th TFW, which managed Korat temporary deployments from 5 April 1965 to 8 April 1966)

13th Tactical Fighter Squadron (May 1966–Oct 1967 – absorbed by 44th TFS)
- 34th Tactical Fighter Squadron (May 1966–May 1969)
- 44th Tactical Fighter Squadron – 21 April – 23 June and 10–29 December 1965, then April 1967–October 1969 (reformed from 421st TFS)
- 421st Tactical Fighter Squadron (April 1966–April 1967 – reformed as 44th TFS)
- 469th Tactical Fighter Squadron – TDY to Kadena 30 November 1964, rotating to Korat 5 January – 13 March 1965. Permanent Change of Station (PCS) to Korat, 6234th TFW on 8 November 1965 as the first F-105 unit in Southeast Asia.

4520th Combat Crew Training Wing, Nellis AFB, Nevada
- 4523rd Combat Crew Training Squadron (1960–1967)
- 4526th Combat Crew Training Squadron (1960–1967)
- 4537th Fighter Weapons Squadron (March 1961–Jun 1968)

US Air Force Reserve:
508th Tactical Fighter Wing, Hill AFB
- 466th Tactical Fighter Squadron (May 1981–Oct 1982). Later became part of the 419th TFW

419th Tactical Fighter Wing, Hill AFB
- 466th Tactical Fighter Squadron (Oct 1982–Feb 1984)

301st Tactical Fighter Wing, Carswell AFB
- 457th Tactical Fighter Squadron (July 1972–Dec 1982)

507th Tactical Fighter Group, Tinker AFB (May 1972–Oct 1980)
- 465th Tactical Fighter Squadron

Air National Guard units:
113th Tactical Fighter Group, District of Columbia ANG, Andrews AFB. Inactivated in December 1974
- 121st Tactical Fighter Squadron (July 1971–July 1981). Assigned 113th Tactical Fighter Wing in December 1974

184th Tactical Fighter Group, Kansas ANG, McConnell AFB
- 127th Tactical Fighter Squadron (Mar 1971–Nov 1979)

116th Tactical Fighter Group, Georgia ANG, Dobbins AFB
- 128th Tactical Fighter Squadron (Aug 1979–Aug 1983)

192nd Tactical Fighter Group, Virginia ANG, Byrd Field ANGB
- 149th Tactical Fighter Squadron (Jan 1971–FY 1982)

Appendix 3 – F-105 Thunderchief tail codes

Tail code	Squadron	Wing	Squadron colour	Base
GA	561 TFS	35 TFW	Yellow	George AFB
GA	562 TFS	35 TFW	Blue	George AFB
GA	563 TFS	35 TFW	Red	George AFB
GR	80 TFS	6441 TFW	Yellow	Yokota AB
HI	466 TFS	508 TFW		Hill AFB
JB	17 WWS	388 TFW		Korat RTAFB
JE	13 TFS	388 TFW		Korat RTAFB
JE	44 TFS	388 TFW	Black	Korat RTAFB
JJ	34 TFS	388 TFW		Korat RTAFB
JV	469 TFS	388 TFW		Korat RTAFB
MD	561 TFS	23 TFW	Yellow	McConnell AFB
MD	561 TFS	23 TFW	Yellow	Korat RTAFB
ME	562 TFS	23 TFW	Blue	McConnell AFB
ME	562 TFS	23 TFW	Blue	Korat RTAFB
MF	563 TFS	23 TFW	Red	McConnell AFB
MF	563 TFS	23 TFW	Red	Korat RTAFB
MG	4519 TFTS	23 TFW		McConnell AFB
NJ	141 TFS	108 TFW	Red	McGuire AFB
RE	44 TFS	355 TFW		Takhli RTAFB
RK	333 TFS	355 TFW	Red	Takhli RTAFB
RM	354 TFS	355 TFW		Takhli RTAFB
RU	357 TFS	355 TFW	Yellow	Takhli RTAFB
SH	465 TFS	301 TFW	Blue	Tinker AFB
TH	457 TFS	301 TFW		Carswell AFB
UC	465 TFS	507 TFG	Blue	Tinker AFB
WA	66 TFS	57 FWW	Yellow/Black	Nellis AFB
WC	4537 TFTS	57 FWW	Yellow/Black	Nellis AFB

WW	*561 TFS*	*388 TFW*		*Yellow*	*Korat RTAFB*
ZA	*12 TFS*	*18 TFW*		*Yellow*	*Kadena AFB*
ZB	*6010 WWS*	*388 TFW*			*Korat RTAFB*

Appendix 4 – F-105 Thunderchief Production Table[1]

Serial Number	Model	Number
54-0098–0099	YF-105A-1-RE	2
54-0100–0103	F-105B 1 RE	4
54-0104	F-105B-5-RE	1
54-0105	JF-105B-1-RE	1
54-0106–0107	F-105B-5-RE	2
54-0108	JF-105B-1-RE	1
54-0109–0110	F-105B-5-RE	2
54-0111	F-105B-5-RE	1
54-0112	JF-105B-2-RE	1
57-5776–5784	F-105B-10-RE	9
57-5785–5802	F-105B-15-RE	18
57-5803–5840	F-105B-20-RE	38
58-1146–1148	F-105D-1-RE	3
58-1149–1173	F-105D-5-RE	25
59-1717–1757	F-105D-5-RE	41
59-1758–1774	F-105D-6-RE	17
59-1817–1826	F-105D-6-RE	10
60-0409–0426	F-105D-6-RE	18
60-0427–0535	F-105D-10-RE	109
60-5374–5385	F-105D-10-RE	12
61-0041–0106	F-105D-15-RE	66
61-0107–0161	F-105D-20-RE	55
61-0162–0220	F-105D-25-RE	59
62-4217–4237	F-105D-25-RE	21
62-4238–4276	F-105D-30-RE	39
62-4277–4411	F-105D-31-RE	135
62-4412–4447	F-105F-1-RE	36
63-8260–8366	F-105F-1-RE	107

Bibliography:

F-105D, F-105F & F-105G Flight Manual, USAF 1970.

F-105F Preliminary Flight Manual, USAF 1964.

T.O. 1F-105D-4 Technical Manual, Illustrated Parts Breakdown, Fairchild Republic Company, 29 April 1966, Change 70 – 1 July 1983.

Rasimus, Ed, *When thunder rolled: An F-105 Pilot over North Vietnam*, Presidio Press, 2003.

Davies, Peter, E., *F-105 Thunderchief Units of the Vietnam War*, Osprey Publishing, 2010.

Davies, Peter, E., *F-105 Thunderchief MiG Killers of the Vietnam War*, Osprey Publishing, 2014.

Anderton, David, *Republic F-105 Thunderchief*, Osprey Publishing, 1983.

Davis, Larry, Menard, David, *Republic F-105 Thunderchief* Warbird Tech Series Vol. 18, Specialty Press, 1988.

Davies, Peter, *F-105 Thunderchief*, Air Vanguard 002, Osprey Publishing, 2012.

Davies, Peter, *F-105 Wild Weasel vs. SA-2 Guideline SAM*, Air Vanguard 002, Osprey Publishing, 2012.

Plunkett, W., Howard, *F-105 Thunderchiefs: A 29-Year Illustrated Operational History*, McFarland, 2008.

---

1   Source: USAF Serials 1946 to 1977, Merseyside Aviation Society, June 1977